Universal Basic Income

M. M. Eboch, Book Editor

GREENHAVEN
PUBLISHING

Published in 2022 by Greenhaven Publishing, LLC
353 3rd Avenue, Suite 255, New York, NY 10010

Articles in Greenhaven Publishing anthologies are often edited for length to meet page requirements. In addition, original titles of these works are changed to clearly present the main thesis and to explicitly indicate the author's opinion. Every effort is made to ensure that Greenhaven Publishing accurately reflects the original intent of the authors. Every effort has been made to trace the owners of the copyrighted material.

Library of Congress Cataloging-in-Publication Data

Names: Eboch, M. M., editor.
Title: Universal basic income / M. M. Eboch, editor.
Description: First Edition. | New York : Greenhaven Publishing, 2022. |
    Series: Introducing issues with opposing viewpoints | Includes
    bibliographical references and index. | Contents: Universal basic income
    | Audience: Ages 12–15 | Audience: Grades 7–9 | Summary: "Anthology of diverse viewpoints exploring the debate surrounding universal basic income"— Provided by publisher.
Identifiers: LCCN 2020051527 | ISBN 9781534508057 (library binding) | ISBN
    9781534508040 (paperback)
Subjects: LCSH: Basic income—Juvenile literature. | Social
    justice—Juvenile literature. | Equality—Juvenile literature.
Classification: LCC HC79.I5 U55 2022 | DDC 331.2/3—dc23
LC record available at https://lccn.loc.gov/2020051527

Manufactured in the United States of America

Website: http://greenhavenpublishing.com

Contents

Foreword

Indulging in a wide spectrum of ideas, beliefs, and perspectives is a critical cornerstone of democracy. After all, it is often debates over differences of opinion, such as whether to legalize abortion, how to treat prisoners, or when to enact the death penalty, that shape our society and drive it forward. Such diversity of thought is frequently regarded as the hallmark of a healthy and civilized culture. As the Reverend Clifford Schutjer of the First Congregational Church in Mansfield, Ohio, declared in a 2001 sermon, "Surrounding oneself with only like-minded people, restricting what we listen to or read only to what we find agreeable is irresponsible. Refusing to entertain doubts once we make up our minds is a subtle but deadly form of arrogance." With this advice in mind, Introducing Issues with Opposing Viewpoints books aim to open readers' minds to the critically divergent views that comprise our world's most important debates.

Introducing Issues with Opposing Viewpoints simplifies for students the enormous and often overwhelming mass of material now available via print and electronic media. Collected in every volume is an array of opinions that captures the essence of a particular controversy or topic. Introducing Issues with Opposing Viewpoints books embody the spirit of nineteenth-century journalist Charles A. Dana's axiom: "Fight for your opinions, but do not believe that they contain the whole truth, or the only truth." Absorbing such contrasting opinions teaches students to analyze the strength of an argument and compare it to its opposition. From this process readers can inform and strengthen their own opinions, or be exposed to new information that will change their minds. Introducing Issues with Opposing Viewpoints is a mosaic of different voices. The authors are statesmen, pundits, academics, journalists, corporations, and ordinary people who have felt compelled to share their experiences and ideas in a public forum. Their words have been collected from newspapers, journals, books, speeches, interviews, and the internet, the fastest growing body of opinionated material in the world.

Introducing Issues with Opposing Viewpoints shares many of the well-known features of its critically acclaimed parent series, Opposing

Viewpoints. The articles allow readers to absorb and compare divergent perspectives. Active reading questions preface each viewpoint, requiring the student to approach the material thoughtfully and carefully. Photographs, charts, and graphs supplement each article. A thorough introduction provides readers with crucial background on an issue. An annotated bibliography points the reader toward articles, books, and websites that contain additional information on the topic. An appendix of organizations to contact contains a wide variety of charities, nonprofit organizations, political groups, and private enterprises that each hold a position on the issue at hand. Finally, a comprehensive index allows readers to locate content quickly and efficiently.

Introducing Issues with Opposing Viewpoints is also significantly different from Opposing Viewpoints. As the series title implies, its presentation will help introduce students to the concept of opposing viewpoints and learn to use this material to aid in critical writing and debate. The series' four-color, accessible format makes the books attractive and inviting to readers of all levels. In addition, each viewpoint has been carefully edited to maximize a reader's understanding of the content. Short but thorough viewpoints capture the essence of an argument. A substantial, thought-provoking essay question placed at the end of each viewpoint asks the student to further investigate the issues raised in the viewpoint, compare and contrast two authors' arguments, or consider how one might go about forming an opinion on the topic at hand. Each viewpoint contains sidebars that include at-a-glance information and handy statistics. A Facts About section located in the back of the book further supplies students with relevant facts and figures.

Following in the tradition of the Opposing Viewpoints series, Greenhaven Publishing continues to provide readers with invaluable exposure to the controversial issues that shape our world. As John Stuart Mill once wrote: "The only way in which a human being can make some approach to knowing the whole of a subject is by hearing what can be said about it by persons of every variety of opinion and studying all modes in which it can be looked at by every character of mind. No wise man ever acquired his wisdom in any mode but this." It is to this principle that Introducing Issues with Opposing Viewpoints books are dedicated.

Introduction

"Every generation expands its definition of equality. Now it's our time to define a new social contract for our generation. We should explore ideas like universal basic income to give everyone a cushion to try new things."

—*Mark Zuckerberg*

How would you like to get a check every month—without having to do anything to earn it? That's what universal basic income (UBI) promises. UBI is *universal* because everyone in a country would get the same amount of money each year. It doesn't matter if someone earned a high income or a low income, or if they didn't work at all. UBI is *basic* because ideally the income would be enough to cover someone's basic needs and allow them to survive without additional income. (In reality, many proposals suggest paying an amount that would still put people well below the poverty line.)

Tech leaders such as Elon Musk of Tesla and Mark Zuckerberg of Facebook support the idea. They say it would help Americans who've been put out of work by automation. Some 25% of US jobs may be lost to automation in the coming years, including jobs in office administration, transportation, production, and food preparation. UBI could help people who lose their jobs go back to school, train for new jobs, or start their own small businesses. In addition, millions of people, mostly women, currently spend their days taking care of children or elderly or infirm family members for free. UBI would pay them for the work they are already doing.

Proponents of UBI say it will have many benefits. It will help keep young people in school longer. It will keep people working because they will be able to train for better, more interesting jobs. UBI will grow the economy by giving people more money to spend. It will improve physical and mental health when people can afford healthier food and the medicine they need. In countries with extreme poverty, it will provide better sanitation, clean water to drink, and enough food. It will help parents afford school fees, so children can stay in school longer.

All those things sound good, and most people wouldn't turn down free money, right? And yet, several European countries have voted down UBI proposals. The concept got some attention in the United States during the 2020 Democratic primary, when candidate Andrew Yang proposed a UBI of $1000 per month for adults over 18. Opponents argued the plan would be too expensive and might even make inequality worse. Most proposed programs use UBI to replace current government programs to help the poor. That helps cut red tape and government waste, but it might also mean poor people receive less help than before. In addition, UBI does not directly address factors that contribute to poverty, such as addiction or lack of skills.

Some opponents also argue that UBI removes the incentive to work. This could hurt the economy, which depends on giving people an incentive to take and keep jobs. Besides, many people believe everyone should work for what they earn. The American dream is an ideal that says everyone has an equal opportunity to achieve success and prosperity by working hard. The idea of giving money to everyone, whether or not they have done anything to earn it, offends many people.

The 2020 Democratic primary went to Joe Biden, who wrote, "Americans have always defined themselves by what they do and how they provide for their families. What the idea of a universal basic income misses is that a job is about more than a paycheck. It is about dignity and one's place in their community. What Americans want is a good job and a steady paycheck, not a government check or a consolation prize for missing out on the American dream." He and most other candidates in the 2020 Democratic primary argued for raising the minimum wage, reforming taxes to let low-income workers keep more of their income, paying for people to go to community college, or guaranteeing jobs for everyone who wants one. These proposals focus on getting people to work, not paying them whether or not they work.

On the surface, it sounds fair to pay people for the work they do rather than give them money for nothing. However, the world doesn't actually work that way now. People who already have money can invest that money and watch it grow. They need to do very little except trust investments to grow over time. Meanwhile, low-income Americans rarely have money to invest. They may struggle to save a few hundred dollars and then see that disappear in unexpected medical bills or car repairs. This pattern means that children who grow up in poverty tend to remain in poverty as adults.

Despite the promises of the American dream, young people from wealthier families have many advantages that put them ahead from the start. They have early intervention for physical or learning challenges, better access to a good education, afterschool programs to explore diverse interests, the funding to go to college, and the social connections to network for jobs. It is one reason more people of color live in poverty. It's a cycle that current government programs have not managed to break.

But would implementing UBI really balance out this inequality? Would it make poverty and inequality better or worse? The problem is, we don't really know. UBI has only been tested in a few small pilot programs. Generally these programs only provided money to the poorest people, so they are not universal. Some programs did not pay enough for a basic income.

Studies showed that people who receive UBI primarily spend money on food, utility bills, and clothes, not alcohol or drugs, as some feared. UBI recipients report less stress and improved mental and physical health. People who receive UBI are happier. The payments don't make people either more or less likely to work. Does this mean UBI was a success or not?

Yang dropped out of the race before the COVID-19 pandemic, which put millions of people out of work through no fault of their own. Would his ideas have been accepted more easily a few months later, when many leaders urged people to stay home for the health and welfare of their country? Should we even be basing our value as human beings on the work we do?

Experts argue about the long-term effects of a true UBI. We may never know, unless countries start providing a UBI. Even then, the effects in India or Kenya may be different from the effects in Great Britain or the United States. The current debates are explored in *Introducing Issues with Opposing Viewpoints: Universal Basic Income*, shedding light on this ongoing contemporary issue.

Chapter 1

What Would Universal Basic Income Do?

Opinions about universal basic income as a solution to income inequality are mixed.

Do you support a universal basic income program?

☐ No

☐ Yes

UBI: The Good, the Bad, and the Complicated

Divakar Shenoy

"As a form of social security UBI will help in reducing inequality and eliminating poverty."

In the following viewpoint, Divakar Shenoy explains the basics of universal basic income, or UBI. Under UBI, everyone would receive the same amount of income from the government. People who have additional income from jobs or other sources would pay taxes on that income. Ideally, the taxes and other government income would pay for UBI. The government would save money by issuing a payment to everyone, rather than spending money trying to determine who needs government help and providing services to them. However, implementing UBI has challenges. This viewpoint was written for Clear IAS, a program to help people study for a civil services exam in India.

"Universal Basic Income (UBI): Everything You Need to Know," Divakar Shenoy, ClearIAS.com. Reference: https://www.clearias.com/universal-basic-income-ubi/

AS YOU READ, CONSIDER THE FOLLOWING QUESTIONS:
1. What is universal basic income?
2. Why does the progression of technology make UBI valuable, according to the author?
3. How are banks and ATMs important if UBI is to work?

Economic Survey for the year 2016–17 has an entire chapter dedicated to the discussion on Universal Basic Income (UBI). In this article let us try to understand the concept of Universal Basic Income, why it is needed, what are the challenges in its implementation and other related issues.

What Is Universal Basic Income (UBI)?

Universal Basic Income is a periodic, unconditional cash transfer to every citizen in the country. Here, social or economic positions of the individual are not taken into consideration. The concept of universal basic income has three main features. They are as following:
1. UBI is universal in nature. It means UBI is not targeted.
2. The second feature of UBI is cash transfer instead of in-kind transfer.
3. The third feature is that UBI is unconditional. That means one need not prove his or her unemployment status or socio-economic identity to be eligible for UBI.

Why Universal Basic Income?

As a form of social security UBI will help in reducing inequality and eliminating poverty. Thus it ensures security and dignity for all individuals. As human labour is being substituted by technology, there will be reduced wage income and reduced purchasing power. UBI will compensate for reduced purchasing power.

How UBI Works

Under UBI, only those with zero income will receive the full benefits in net terms. For those who earn additional income over the basic income, the net benefits will taper off through taxation. So even though the basic income is universal, only the poor will receive the full benefits.

What UBI Means to the Government
There would be drastic changes in the way government spends its revenue generated from taxation and other sources. Currently, government spends its revenue on various services as well as on subsidies. UBI would mean that government may move away from service delivery and empower its citizens to access services through cash transfer.

What Are the Advantages of UBI?
First, UBI would give individuals freedom to spend the money in a way they choose. In other words, UBI strengthens economic liberty at an individual level. This would help them to choose the kind of work they want to do, rather than forcing them to do unproductive work to meet their daily requirements.

Universal Basic Income would be a sort of an insurance against unemployment and hence helps in reducing poverty.

UBI will result in equitable distribution of wealth. As explained above, only the poor will receive the full net benefits.

Increased income will increase the bargaining power of individuals, as they will no longer be forced to accept any working conditions.

UBI is easy to implement. Because of its universal character, there is no need to identify the beneficiaries. Thus it excludes errors in identifying the intended beneficiaries—which is a common problem in targeted welfare schemes.

As every individual receives basic income, it promotes efficiency by reducing wastages in government transfers. This would also help in reducing corruption.

Considerable gains could be achieved in terms of bureaucratic costs and time by replacing many of the social sector schemes with UBI.

As the economic survey points out, transferring basic income directly into bank accounts will increase the demand for financial services. This would help banks to invest in the expansion of their service network, which is very important for financial inclusion.

Advocates claim that UBI would reduce the need for government entitlement programs.

Under some circumstances, UBI could promote greater productivity. For example, agriculture labourers who own a small patch of land and earlier used to work in others' farms for low wages can now undertake farming on their own land. In the long term, this will reduce the percentage of unused land and help in increasing agriculture productivity.

What Are the Main Arguments Against UBI?

A guaranteed minimum income might make people lazy and it breeds dependency. They may opt out of the labour market.

There is no guarantee that the additional income will be spent on education, health etc. There are chances that the money will be spent on "temptation goods" such as alcohol, tobacco, drugs etc.

Given the large population size, the fiscal burden on government would be high. Also, as Economic Survey 2016–17 noted, once implemented, it may become difficult for the government to end UBI in the case of failure.

If the UBI is funded by higher taxes, especially by the indirect taxes, it will result in inflation. This, in turn, will reduce the purchasing power of the people and lower the value of the amount transferred.

A "guaranteed minimum income" might reduce the availability of workers in some sectors which are necessary but unattractive and raise the wages of such works. For example, the wages of agriculture labourers might increase due to non-availability of workers willing to work in others' farms.

What Are the Challenges That May Come from Implementation of UBI?

According to the World Bank, in India, there are only 20 ATMs for every [100,000 adults]. Nearly one-third of Indian adults remain unbanked. With such a state of financial service infrastructure and financial inclusion, it would be difficult for the people to access their benefits.

Financing the "guaranteed minimum income" would be another challenge. There are chances that UBI would become an add-on to existing subsidies rather than replace them.

What Economic Survey 2016–17 Says About UBI

The Economic Survey 2016–17 assumes that in practice any program cannot strive for strict universality. So the survey proposes some alternatives:

- First, the survey targets the bottom 75 percent of the population and this is termed "quasi-universality." The cost for this quasi-universality is estimated to be around 4.9 percent of GDP.
- A second alternative targets women, who generally face worse prospects in employment opportunities, education, health or financial inclusion. A UBI for women can reduce the fiscal cost of providing a UBI to about half. Giving money to women also reduces the concerns of money being used on "temptation goods."
- Third, to start with a UBI for certain vulnerable groups such as widows, pregnant mothers, the old and the infirm.

But, if any one of the above alternatives is adopted, it will also face the problem of "exclusion error" in the identification of beneficiaries. Efficiency will be reduced. Corruption will creep in. More importantly, UBI will not remain "universal."

UBI and "JAM Trinity"

JAM is the short form of Jan Dhan, Aadhaar, Mobile. Currently, there are 26.5 crore [265,000,000] Jan Dhan [bank] accounts across the country. This covers 21 percent of the population. Of these accounts, 57 percent are Aadhaar [unique identity number] seeded. Over a billion Aadhaar cards have been distributed.

When the trinity of Jan Dhan, Aadhaar, and Mobile (popularly referred to as JAM) is fully adopted, a more efficient mode of delivery would be available.

The JAM system could be used to provide funds to each individual directly into his or her account.

The Main Problems in the "JAM Trinity"

Authentication failures in Aadhaar are as high as 49 percent in Jharkhand. This will result in the exclusion of beneficiaries.

A large number of Jan Dhan accounts are not active. According to Financial Inclusion Insights (FII-2015), only 40 percent of the accounts are active. Still, nearly one-third of Indian adults remained unbanked. There are issues in mobile network connectivity, especially in rural India.

UBI in Other Parts of the World

Finland has started a pilot programme this year to understand the effects of a basic income. The Finland government would pay €560 per month to two thousand unemployed individuals for the next two years, and it would continue to provide the income even if individuals find employment during this period.

Some regions in the Netherlands and Canada have also announced a pilot programme.

But, last year, Switzerland voted on UBI and rejected the proposal to transfer 2,500 Swiss francs per month to every adult citizen and long-term resident. The fiscal implication was the main reason for rejection of the proposal in Switzerland.

Conclusion

Despite making remarkable progress in poverty reduction, nearly 22 percent of the population lives below the poverty line (Tendulkar committee report, 2011–12). One of the major criticisms of poverty alleviation programmes is significant leakages. UBI is seen as a more efficient alternative.

Though UBI has many advantages, there are many practical challenges too. A transparent and safe financial architecture that is accessible to all is important for the success of the UBI. In other words, the success of UBI depends on the success of an efficient mode of delivery like JAM Trinity.

Also, a behavioral change on the part of account holders is needed so that they use their accounts more often. Banks need to find it profitable to provide access to banking services.

As the economic survey states, UBI is a powerful idea whose time even if not ripe for implementation is ripe for serious discussion

EVALUATING THE AUTHOR'S ARGUMENTS:

Viewpoint author Divakar Shenoy lists advantages and challenges to universal basic income. Do you think the author has a personal opinion about whether UBI should be implemented? Why do you think that?

Viewpoint 2

First Decide the Goal of UBI

André Gonçalves

"You might claim it is a utopian view but many experts will likely tell you all great ideas we have today were once revolutionary and judged as crazy."

In the following viewpoint, André Gonçalves debates some pros and cons of UBI. He notes that some early test programs have had positive results. However, they weren't necessarily the results expected or desired. In order to determine whether UBI is successful, we first need to define what success means. Is it a stronger economy, lower unemployment, more leisure time, or happiness? UBI might be effective in improving some of these areas but not all of them. André Gonçalves studied sustainability management in Portugal. He is an editor for Youmatter, a website to inform, explain, and accelerate positive change.

"Universal Basic Income: Is It Utopian Giving Free Money to Everyone?" by André Gonçalves, youmatter, June 24, 2019. Reprinted by permission.

AS YOU READ, CONSIDER THE FOLLOWING QUESTIONS:
1. How would UBI affect the arts, according to the author?
2. Do people who get UBI spend the money on drugs and alcohol, according to sources cited?
3. What did the Finland study show in terms of happiness for the people involved?

What is the definition of universal basic income? Why did it become so popular all of a sudden? How realistic is it? Won't people stop working once they get paid for no reason? Let's find out.

Universal Basic Income: How It Became Mainstream

There's a particularly interesting World Economic Forum's Annual Meeting that took place in Davos (as usual) in 2019. The purpose of that year's conference was to discuss how to improve our societies and design a better version of globalization. Apart from some news questioning how eco-friendly the business and government leaders flying there in private jets was, everything was going reasonably normal. At least until the Dutch historian showed up.

The video of Rutger Bregman saying he felt like he was at "a fire-fighters conference and no one was allowed to speak about water" went viral in the days following the conference. Bregman was expected to contribute to the panel discussion on inequality by adding the perspective of universal basic income (UBI). Instead, as he recently told Trevor Noah on the *Daily Show*, the fact that days had gone by and "everyone was avoiding to talk about the T-word," i.e., taxes and tax avoidance, the historian decided to go for a quite controversial speech.

However, a universal basic income was far from being a new idea, despite its popularity rise over the last years and now in 2020 because of the effects of the new coronavirus is having on the economy.

Some pilot tests have been implemented across the world in specific regions within countries like Finland (whose 2 year program recently ended), the Netherlands, Italy, Canada, Uganda, Kenya and India—we will review their results. Moreover, one of the former candidates to represent the democratic party in the 2020 United States election, Andrew Yang, was delivering the promise of giving US$1000 per month to every American if he got elected president. But what is a universal basic income after all?

What Is a Universal Basic Income? UBI Definition

What is the definition of a universal basic income? A basic income is a policy where citizens get a certain amount of money during a determined period, with no strings attached. Individuals don't have to work to earn it and they can spend it however they want to. Everyone gets the same no matter what their gender, family structure, housing costs or employment status is. Make this a national (or even global) policy and you'll get to the concept of universal basic income.

Some well-known figures have in fact discussed or supported the idea of adopting a universal basic income. From the British philosopher Thomas More (who wrote the famous book *Utopia* in the 16th century) and the economist and Nobel Prize winner Milton Friedman, to Martin Luther King, the former US president Barack Obama and the business entrepreneur from Tesla and Space-X, Elon Musk.

The Benefits of a Society with a Universal Basic Income

UBI supporters stand upon different arguments to sustain the need to think about developing universal basic income policies. One of the strongest has to do with the fact that AI and automation is coming and between 400 million to 800 million jobs worldwide might be automated by 2030. Moreover, 75 million to 375 million may need to switch occupational categories and learn new skills, according to McKinsey. In this way, the tech-caused unemployment argument defends UBI as a way of transition to a society where people work more on a part-time basis and have more spare time.

All this, while getting a certain amount of money. It can also be useful, according to Yuval Noah Hariri, the author of the famous book *Sapiens*, as a way of making sure people get a living during a transition period. The Israeli says people will need to develop new hard skills to work in a mostly tech-based job market as their jobs get

The concept of UBI is more nuanced than many people understand. It would not be throwing free money at people.

increasingly automated. During this adaptation period, people might need a UBI that guarantees their livelihood.

Then there's also the argument that apart from this transition role, a universal basic income would also help fight many of today's economic problems. That's why economists and policy analysts are interested in how UBI would affect, apart from employment, society as a whole. They are particularly interested in the effects a universal basic income would have on people's sense of security regarding their income, according to O'Malley's and Rothstein's report on UBI in the US and other advanced countries.

A universal basic income might, for instance, increase the bargaining power of workers by leaving them more comfortable to look for fairer working conditions. Furthermore, a basic income of USD $12,000/year for every American would make the economy grow around 13% by 2025, according to data from the Roosevelt Institute.

And what if—you might claim it is a utopian view but many experts will likely tell you all great ideas we have today were once revolutionary and judged as crazy—people started leaving their unpleasant jobs? They would have more time to dedicate to, for instance, art activities such as music or painting, or even risk opening their own companies, developing recreative communities... simply because they would have a UBI backup in case things go wrong? In times of quarantine with people all over the world staying home, we remember the important of the artists who produced the books we read, the movies we watch or the songs we listen to.

This space to dedicate to arts could improve both people's well-being and their entrepreneurial mindset. And it seems to be what happened in Finland, where despite the fact employment didn't improve, the life quality of the participants did. Poverty was eradicated and entrepreneurship got a boost. This is not to speak of hypothetical improvements in health, especially due to depression reduction. Furthermore, Bregman defends people might even get smarter as they overcome their mental scarcity. Some studies suggest it might lead to a 13 IQ points increase.

Concerns on Universal Basic Income

But won't people stop working? you might ask. It is still too early to tell with certainty. But a 2016 study suggests this is not the case and that transfer programs won't discourage people from working. At the same time, a universal basic income wouldn't likely be a great salary that would allow excessive consumption or some luxury. The people getting them would still need to work to have the chance of enjoying expensive experiences and buying products.

There are also the worries that a universal basic income is spent on drugs and alcohol. The same study from above also says there's no significant connection between money transfers and an increase in the consumption of goods such as alcohol and tobacco. In fact, according to Bregman's book *Utopia for Realists*, poor people in countries like Kenya and Uganda used their money wisely and even got to improve the living conditions in their villages. Moreover, according to a study from the University of Manchester, programs like the universal basic income will likely mean households will put their money to good use and poverty will likely decline.

Another concern or motive for disagreement is perhaps the fact that, for instance, in the US, many people still don't have basic literacy skills while others struggle at completing basic financial forms. Would these people be able to innovate and improve their lives all alone? Perhaps not. Perhaps they would still need some assistance.

And what about those who don't need the money? Is it fair that rich people get the same share of money and contribute to emptying the funds from which the money comes from? Is it fair that a UBI replaces medical and social securities (because states give people their welfare money and stop providing these services over all) and young people who have less health problems take money from the same cake as old people, even though they won't probably need so much assistance? Or the opposite for education expenses.

Should We Continue Assessing the Potential of a Universal Basic Income?

The paper from O'Malley and Rothstein suggests the ongoing pilot studies need some adjustments in order to be truly effective and give valuable insights about the relevance of developing universal basic policies. Specifically, the authors say it's important to define better what would be a positive outcome of a UBI pilot, which doesn't necessarily have to do exclusively with UBI.

Do we effectively want to increase employment? Because the Finish study will say UBI didn't work for them. Or do we expect UBI to leave people happier? Because it indeed happened in Finland. What social ills do we want to fix? Do we want people to improve the resilience of their local system? Because that seemed to be what happened in African countries.

Do we have a common, widespread vision where people will work less (as an effect of automation and economic wealth that's fairly distributed) and dedicate more time to their education, to develop creativity or to design solutions to fight climate change? Perhaps a world where people meditate more often and can learn to control the responses of their autononous nervous systems and enhance their immunity?

O'Malley and Rothstein suggest that, right now, UBI is proposed as a solution to many different social ills and its details are often underspecified—so it's not clear who'd get money, how much, or how it would be funded. So questions like how a universal basic income would fit with existing programs (or replace them?) and how nations would pay for it requires holistic answers backed up with realistic solutions.

In the end, we can say more experiments will probably need to be done to assess whether a universal basic income would be a good idea. But before running these studies, different actors of society need to agree on and co-design what a better future would look like. Otherwise, assessing the impacts of new policies without having agreed on the desired outcome may just be a waste of time. And money.

EVALUATING THE AUTHOR'S ARGUMENTS:

Viewpoint author André Gonçalves writes that we should determine what results we want from UBI before going any further. He lists several possibilities. What would you expect to see if UBI passed in your country? Which goals would be most important to you? Why?

UBI Overcomes the Limitations of Targeted Basic Income

"UBI is not a new concept, but it is a concept which has taken the world by storm in the recent years."

IANS

In the following viewpoint, IANS discusses a UBI program intended for Sikkim, a state in northeastern India. Political parties in Sikkim had different views about implementing a basic income program. The author argues that UBI would be more efficient and effective than a targeted basic income program, which would only apply to the poorest people. The author also claims UBI is especially valuable to young people. IANS is a member of Parliament and a spokesperson for the Sikkim Democratic Front political party.

"Sikkim Will Be First State to Implement Universal Basic Income; It's Different from Congress' NYAY (Comment)," by IANS, Business Standard Private Ltd., March 29, 2019. Reprinted by permission.

AS YOU READ, CONSIDER THE FOLLOWING QUESTIONS:
1. What is the difference between UBI and targeted basic income?
2. How does targeted basic income encourage corruption, according to the viewpoint?
3. What government income would help pay for UBI, according to the author?

On January 10, 2019, the SDF party announced in the national media that we would be implementing Universal Basic Income (UBI) in Sikkim by 2022. Following this, there has been an explosion of media coverage on UBI. It received coverage in all national media and even international media, including the *Washington Post* and the *Strait Times*.

UBI is a basic income and can be defined as a modest amount of money paid unconditionally to all individuals on a regular basis (for example, monthly). It is popularly known as Universal Basic Income because it is intended to pay all individuals regardless of income, with no spending conditions and no behavioural requirements. This non-withdrawable and non-repayable income is to provide basic income security to all, especially to the most insecure groups in society. This vision was also reaffirmed by Sikkim Chief Minister Pawan Chamling in a press release on March 27, 2019.

Bhaichung Bhutia also announced on March 26 that the opposition Hamro Sikkim Party (HSP) would also implement Universal Basic Income in Sikkim, calling it "Sikkim Samman Yojana." However, it would only be for households where the monthly income is less than Rs 25,000. This is not "universal" basic income, but targeted basic income.

This is more aligned with Congress President Rahul

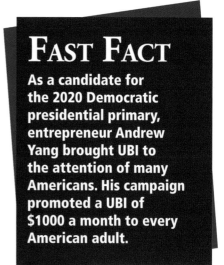

FAST FACT

As a candidate for the 2020 Democratic presidential primary, entrepreneur Andrew Yang brought UBI to the attention of many Americans. His campaign promoted a UBI of $1000 a month to every American adult.

Proponents believe that UBI would benefit young people because it would provide security for an uncertain future in which technology might eliminate many job opportunities.

Gandhi's version of basic income guarantee or Nyunatam Aay Yojana (NYAY), which was announced by Congress on March 25 and said that the party would provide minimum basic income to the poorest 20 per cent category. There are many criticisms associated with targeted basic income. The most salient of these is that it creates a fertile breeding ground for corruption since bureaucrats have the discretionary powers to either include or exclude people. The other is that it stigmatises the recipients who need to prove that they are eligible for support.

However, the very logic behind SDF's promise of UBI is that by being universal and unconditional it overcomes these limitations and creates a transparent system of transferring cash to people directly at almost negligible administrative cost. Moreover, it doesn't stigmatise the recipient. This is wholly driven by SDF's pro-poor, youth-centric, sustainability-driven ideology. Our version of UBI is different from what has been promised by Bhaichung Bhutia and Rahul Gandhi. Ours is not a yojana—yojana would mean that it comes with a fixed time period. Our version of UBI is aimed at serving Sikkim and its people for times to come. We aim to make it a sustainable system which can run beyond our years. Ours is an income—not a grant. Ours is truly universal—with no discrimination based on income, age, background, etc.

With new technologies, robots, artificial intelligence, etc., a lot of jobs are evaporating. We believe that one way to secure the future of our youth is through UBI which promises a regular stipend. This would open up a lot of opportunities for our youth to make certain choices about their future—it would give them a secure financial cushion. This is why we have said that UBI is youth-centric programme. It is in a way going to future-proof our youth.

Bhutia in his press conference said that this scheme hasn't been tried anywhere in India, however, UBI has already been implemented successfully in pilot projects in Madhya Pradesh and Gujarat. These are well-documented cases. UBI is not a new concept, but it is a concept which has taken the world by storm in the recent years. Andy Yang, one of the contestants for the 2020 US presidential elections has already announced a UBI plan for the US. Therefore, UBI is not a new concept. This is a powerful idea which has the power to transform lives and make them more secure and to turn society into a more humane one. The time for UBI is now.

UBI is, however, a giant leap of faith, as has been articulated by the CM. It will require a lot of government motivation and willpower to successfully implement this scheme. I believe an experienced and motivated party like SDF will be able to deliver on this. We are in touch with the leading thinkers on this issue and we have a protracted programme of consultation with the people of Sikkim. Through a participatory approach we will make this work. We will be creating a Sikkim Dividend Fund (SDF) by an act of the state assembly. This dividend fund will be created as a corpus through which we will be able to make the payments without any hassle. In addition to the money from natural resources, revenue from other economic activities like tourism will be used to fund this programme. Some of the already institutionalised schemes may be subsumed into this.

SDF has thought this through as a programme which will continue to serve the generations to come. Given that poverty in Sikkim is almost negligible, UBI will help in bringing equity and establish a common minimum floor for all Sikkimese people. For Bhutia's HSP UBI is a poll promise; for SDF it comes from our ideological roots and is part of our youth-first programme.

EVALUATING THE AUTHOR'S ARGUMENTS:

This viewpoint was written by someone associated with a political party. Do you see indications that the author is pushing a particular viewpoint? What wording gives you clues? Is the argument effective? Why or why not?

UBI Might Solve the Problems Automation Brings

"There is a pretty good chance we end up with a universal basic income, or something like that, due to automation."

Neyaz Farooquee

In the following article, Neyaz Farooquee discusses the potential for unemployment due to automation. The Industrial Revolution brought changes to the kinds of work people do. Recent technology, including artificial intelligence (AI), has sped up the rate of change. Many people will find their jobs obsolete in a few years. Other workers may need to constantly scramble to learn new skills in order to keep up with job demands. The author suggests that UBI may be a way to offset joblessness and poverty. Neyaz Farooquee is a journalist based in Delhi, India.

AS YOU READ, CONSIDER THE FOLLOWING QUESTIONS:
1. How will automation affect jobs, according to the viewpoint?
2. How does technology affect the speed at which people need to learn new skills?
3. How might AI cause a greater gap between the rich and poor, according to the author?

Automation is here on us, and, in the years to come, Artificial Intelligence (AI) will take it to an unprecedented level. It will bring about a profound change in the way we live and earn our livelihood. According to McKinsey, it can potentially leave 800 million of us jobless by 2030 across the world. The situation may be all the more alarming in developing countries; 69% of jobs in India risk losing their relevance in the same period.

That's a scary possibility, given a highly unequal distribution of technological resources. Industry leaders whose innovations will likely influence the AI-related developments suggest Universal Basic Income (UBI) as a solution. For example, Elon Musk told CNBC: "There is a pretty good chance we end up with a universal basic income, or something like that, due to automation." Mark Zuckerberg said during his Harvard commencement speech: "Every generation expands its definition of equality. Now it's our time to define a new social contract for our generation. We should explore ideas like universal basic income to give everyone a cushion to try new things."

In India, the opposition Congress party has announced that it will provide a basic minimum income guarantee to the poor, and the ruling Bharatiya Janata Party has similar ideas to offer. Such schemes are bound to bring immense pressure on the exchequer in their present forms. But, has the Indian political class unintentionally ended up providing a dress rehearsal for a future in which we are likely to face a permanent class of jobless people, in need of state support for survival?

When the machine came with the industrial revolution, it democratised the work culture to a large extent, weakening the institutions of slavery and caste, and making it unavoidable for the rest to work for subsistence. But for the first time in history, humans are facing an existential dilemma, where a substantial number of us stare at the prospect of being jobless because AI doesn't only make humans' physical work irrelevant, it also challenges the human brain, and it will only get better at it with time.

There may be newer job avenues with the proliferation of AI, but it would also mean that to keep themselves employed, humans would have to continuously update their skills. "A generation ago, the half-life of a skill was about 26 years, and that was the model for a career. Today, it's four and half years and dropping," Indranil Roy, the head of the Deloitte's Future of Work Centre of Excellence, told the BBC.

But we are not prepared—emotionally, mentally and in terms of infrastructure—to adapt to such changes so quickly, threatening a prospect of great unpredictability around employment. Among the sectors that are likely to remain relevant—with constant training, of course—are creative, cognitive and technological, but for a large section of workers, it won't be easy keeping up with these.

The possibilities of AI are, however, endless. It can open up jobs that are beyond our imagination right now, and may as well offset the loss in jobs. But the worrisome fact is that it can equally lead to an unprecedented inequality where the haves, having AI (like developed countries and a few individuals like Zuckerberg), will keep growing at a rate which have-nots will never be able to achieve. It may herald an age in which, initially, there is an unprecedented growth but little rise in pay or employment. Eventually, AI-driven automation will cheapen products, resulting in a decline in the wage of leftover jobs, and stagnation in the economy and employment—and could lead to the market's collapse. UBI, in this context, makes business sense to keep the economy running.

Dutch historian Rutger Bregman calls basic income "the venture capital for the people." It could compensate for the loss in jobs and skills, and also help in innovation. Multiple surveys suggest that the young in this age do not recall their working hours as their happiest memories; maybe,

FAST FACT

A generation ago, the skills a worker needed would last them about 26 years on average. Today, it's four and a half years and dropping, according to the Deloitte's Future of Work Centre of Excellence.

While robots and other forms of automation have steadily changed the labor market over the years, advancements in technology and AI are projected to eliminate many more jobs.

the UBI-funded creativity pursuits might help better our happiness index. Many consider George Orwell and Harper Lee, among others, as successes who were provided with basic support.

For many, such possibilities may simply be a red herring. But even if we discount the possibility of a loss in employment, certain activities would undoubtedly become automated (about half of the present-day skills, McKinsey, 2018), making a lot of workers easily dispensable, again leading to lesser pay for the rest of the employed—or pay polarisation, resulting into immense income inequality.

People cried wolf that machines and computers would eat up their jobs. But for the first time in history, it's not just that humans' physical power is being challenged, but also their thinking power, which was unique to humans. Precedence shows that the fallout of shifting from an Industrial and IT age to Artificial Intelligence age would indeed mean loss of jobs—for example, AT&T, worth $267 billion in today's valuation, employed more than 7.5 lakh [750,000] people in 1967, Google, worth $370 billion, employs merely 55,000.

It increasingly appears that the news of the wolf's arrival may not be too far. UBI can become part of the solution, more so in developing countries such as India.

EVALUATING THE AUTHOR'S ARGUMENTS:

According to viewpoint author Neyaz Farooquee, UBI could offset the joblessness and poverty brought on by automation. What evidence does the author use to support these claims? Does this add up to a strong case for UBI, or might there be other options? If so, what are some examples?

Viewpoint

5

UBI Will Increase Poverty, Not Reduce It

"A UBI that's financed primarily by tax increases would require the American people to accept a level of taxation that vastly exceeds anything in US history."

Robert Greenstein

In the following excerpted viewpoint, Robert Greenstein argues that attempts to implement UBI would be quixotic, or idealistic and impractical. So far as UBI has support from the political right, conservatives want to fund UBI by cutting all other government assistance. This could mean far smaller benefits to people in poverty. It is easier to find support for programs such as food stamps and early childhood education. Many Americans do not want money to go to healthy adults who are not working. Robert Greenstein is founder and president of the Center on Budget and Policy Priorities.

"Commentary: Universal Basic Income May Sound Attractive but, If It Occurred, Would Likelier Increase Poverty Than Reduce It," by Robert Greenstein, Center on Budget and Policy Priorities, June 13, 2019. Reprinted by permission.

AS YOU READ, CONSIDER THE FOLLOWING QUESTIONS:
1. Why can Americans not count on taxes to pay for UBI, according to the author?
2. How does "the right" (conservative politicians) want to finance UBI?
3. Would replacing current programs for low-income families with a modest UBI provide more or less money, according to the viewpoint?

At first blush, universal basic income (UBI) seems a very attractive idea, especially to a progressive. Yet it suffers from two serious problems. First, the odds are very high that an effort to secure UBI would prove quixotic. Second, and more disconcerting, any possibility of overcoming the formidable obstacles to UBI will almost certainly require a left-right coalition that has significant conservative support—and conservative support for UBI rests on an approach that would increase poverty, rather than reduce it.

The key issues related to UBI include what it would cost, how it would be paid for, and the risks it poses. Let's take these one at a time.

The Cost

There are over 300 million Americans today. Suppose UBI provided everyone with $10,000 a year. That would cost more than $3 trillion a year—and $30 trillion to $40 trillion over ten years.

This single-year figure equals more than three-fourths of the entire yearly federal budget—and double the entire budget outside Social Security, Medicare, defense, and interest payments. It's also equal to close to 100 percent of all tax revenue the federal government collects.

Or, consider UBI that gives everyone $5,000 a year. That would provide income equal to about two-fifths of the poverty line for an individual (which is a projected $12,700 in 2016) and less than the poverty line for a family of four ($24,800). But it would cost as

Would UBI eliminate much needed assistance such as important school lunch programs?

much as the entire federal budget outside Social Security, Medicare, defense, and interest payments.

Some UBI proponents respond that policymakers could make the UBI payments taxable. But the savings from doing so would be relatively modest, because the vast bulk of Americans either owe no federal income tax or are in the 10% or 15% tax brackets. For example, if you gave all 328 million Americans a $10,000 UBI and the cost was $3.28 trillion a year (about $33 trillion over ten years) before taxes, then making the UBI payments taxable would reduce that cost only to something like $2.5 trillion or $2.75 trillion (or $25 trillion to $27.5 trillion over ten years).

Paying for It

Where would the money to finance such a large expenditure come from? That it would come mainly or entirely from new taxes isn't plausible. We'll already need substantial new revenues in the coming decades to help keep Social Security and Medicare solvent and avoid large benefit cuts in them. We'll need further tax increases to help repair a crumbling infrastructure that will otherwise impede economic

FAST FACT

The population of the United States is over 330 million. If UBI provided everyone with $10,000 a year, that would cost more than $3 trillion a year.

growth. And if we want to create more opportunity and reduce racial and other barriers and inequities, we'll also need to raise new revenues to invest more in areas like pre-school education, child care, college affordability, and revitalizing segregated inner-city communities.

A UBI that's financed primarily by tax increases would require the American people to accept a level of taxation that vastly exceeds anything in US history. It's hard to imagine that such a UBI would advance very far, especially given the tax increases we'll already need for Social Security, Medicare, infrastructure, and other needs.

The Risk

UBI's daunting financing challenges raise fundamental questions about its political feasibility, both now and in coming decades. Proponents often speak of an emerging left-right coalition to support it. But consider what UBI's supporters on the right advocate. They generally propose UBI as a replacement for the current "welfare state." That is, they would finance UBI by eliminating all or most programs for people with low or modest incomes.

Consider what that would mean. If you take the dollars targeted on people in the bottom fifth or two-fifths of the population and convert them to universal payments to people all the way up the income scale, you're redistributing income upward. That would increase poverty and inequality rather than reduce them.

Yet that's the platform on which the (limited) support for UBI on the right largely rests. It entails abolishing programs from SNAP (food stamps)—which largely eliminated the severe child malnutrition found in parts of the Southern "black belt" and Appalachia in the late 1960s—to the Earned Income Tax Credit (EITC), Section 8 rental vouchers, Medicaid, Head Start, child care assistance, and many others. These programs lift tens of millions of people, including millions of children, out of poverty each year and make tens of millions more less poor.

Some UBI proponents may argue that by ending current programs, we'd reap large administrative savings that we could convert into UBI payments. But that's mistaken. For the major means-tested programs—SNAP, Medicaid, the EITC, housing vouchers, Supplemental Security Income (SSI), and school meals—administrative costs consume only 1 to 9 percent of program resources, as a CBPP analysis explains.[1] Their funding goes overwhelmingly to boost the incomes and purchasing power of low-income families.

Moreover, as the Roosevelt Institute's Mike Konczal has noted, eliminating Medicaid, SNAP, the EITC, housing vouchers, and the like would still leave you far short of what's needed to finance a meaningful UBI.[2] Would we also end Pell Grants that help low-income students afford college? Would we terminate support for children in foster care, for mental health services, and for job training?

Ed Dolan, who favors UBI, has calculated that we could finance it by using the proceeds from eliminating all means-tested programs outside health care—including Pell Grants, job training, Head Start, free school lunches, and the like, as well as refundable tax credits, SNAP, SSI, low-income housing programs, etc. The result, Dolan found, would be an annual UBI of $1,582 per person, well below the level of support most low-income families (especially working-poor families with children) now receive. The increase in poverty and hardship would be very large.[3]

That's why the risk is high that under any UBI that could conceivably gain traction politically, tens of millions of poor people would likely end up worse off.

To further understand the risks, consider how working-age adults who aren't working would fare. In our political culture, there are formidable political obstacles to providing cash to working-age people who aren't employed, and it's unlikely that UBI could surmount them. The nation's social insurance programs—Social Security, Medicare, and unemployment insurance—all go only to people with significant work records. It's highly unlikely that policymakers would agree to make UBI cash payments of several thousand dollars to people who aren't elderly or disabled and aren't working. (By contrast, there is political support for providing poor families that have no earnings with non-cash assistance such as

SNAP, Medicaid, rental vouchers, Head Start, and the WIC nutrition program.)

[...]

Conclusion

I greatly admire the commitment of UBI supporters who see it as a way to end poverty in America. But for UBI to do that, it would have to: (1) be large enough to raise people to the poverty line without ending Medicaid, child care assistance, assistance in meeting high rental costs, and the like (otherwise, out-of-pocket health, child care, and housing costs would push many people back into poverty); and (2) include among its recipients people who aren't currently working (and lack much of an earnings record), something no US universal program does. It also would have to be financed mainly by raising taxes layered on top of the large tax increases we'll already need—and will probably have to fight tough political battles to achieve—to avert large benefit cuts in Social Security and Medicare and meet other needs.

The chances that all this will come to pass—whether now or 10 to 20 years from now, a time when the baby-boomers will nearly all be retired and Social Security and Medicare costs will be much higher, placing greater pressure on the rest of the budget and on taxes—are extremely low. Were we starting from scratch—and were our political culture more like Western Europe's—UBI might be a real possibility. But that's not the world we live in.

End Notes

1. Robert Greenstein and CBPP staff, "Romney's Charge That Most Federal Low-Income Spending Goes for 'Overhead' and 'Bureaucrats' Is False," updated January 23, 2012, http://www.cbpp.org/research/romneys-charge-that-most-federal-low-income-spending-goes-for-overhead-and-bureaucrats-is?fa=view&id=3655.

2. Mike Konczal, "The Pragmatic Libertarian Case for a Basic Income Doesn't Add Up," Roosevelt Institute, August 8, 2014, http://rooseveltinstitute.org/pragmatic-libertarian-case-basic-income-doesnt-add/.

3. Dolan notes that the UBI could be raised to $3,591 per person if policymakers also entirely eliminated an array of what he calls "middle class tax expenditures"—include the mortgage interest deduction, all tax benefits for 401(k)s, IRAs, and other retirement saving, the deduction for charitable contributions, other individual tax expenditures, and the personal exemption—without lowering tax rates. The chances of policymakers doing that are essentially zero. http://www.economonitor.com/dolanecon/2014/01/13/could-we-afford-a-universal-basic-income/

EVALUATING THE AUTHOR'S ARGUMENTS:

In this viewpoint, Robert Greenstein doesn't question the benefits of UBI. Rather, he questions whether Americans would be willing to accept the changes that would make the program possible in this country. Do you agree with the author's conclusions? Why could it be harder in America than in some other countries?

Chapter 2

What Are the Advantages and Disadvantages of UBI?

Could UBI offset the economic effects of a disaster like the COVID-19 pandemic?

UBI Could Greatly Benefit Families

Clifton B. Parker

"Poverty actually makes it harder to be responsible, to plan, to think about the future."

In the following viewpoint, Clifton B. Parker interviews Jennifer Burns, who discusses the history of UBI and offers an opinion on whether it could work today. Burns notes that the concept is not new: famous economist Milton Friedman suggested something similar in 1939. While UBI could help low-income workers and encourage stronger families, strong national leadership is required to implement it. It is likely that UBI programs would happen at the state level before occurring at the federal level. Clifton B. Parker is former director of Public Policy Communications at Stanford University's Hoover Institution. Jennifer Burns is a research fellow at the Hoover Institution and associate professor of history at Stanford.

"Stanford Scholar Explores Pros, Cons of 'Basic Income,'" by Clifton B. Parker, Stanford University, August 8, 2018. Reprinted by permission.

AS YOU READ, CONSIDER THE FOLLOWING QUESTIONS:
1. When do most welfare programs start providing benefits to people?
2. What is the advantage to giving people cash rather than specific benefits such as food stamps?
3. How does poverty make it difficult for people to be responsible, according to the viewpoint?

G iven the flux of American politics right now, an idea like "universal basic income" could gain political traction, a Stanford historian says.

Stanford scholar Jennifer Burns, a research fellow at the Hoover Institution and an associate professor of history in the Stanford School of Humanities and Sciences, says such a program could help protect workers who hit rock bottom in an age of technological disruption.

A basic income—also called basic income guarantee, universal basic income or basic living stipend—is a program in which citizens of a country receive a regular sum of money from the government. Tech leaders Elon Musk and Mark Zuckerberg have floated the idea, and the city of Chicago is considering such a proposal as a way to reduce the disruptions of automation in the workforce.

Burns researches and writes about 20th-century American intellectual, political, and cultural history and is currently writing a book about the economist Milton Friedman, who supported the idea of a universal income.

What would be the benefits of a universal basic income if it were to become a reality?

The most attractive aspect of universal basic income, or UBI, is that it can serve to underwrite market participation, in contrast to other welfare programs that essentially require people to not be employed to receive the benefit. Some programs even require participants to have essentially zero assets in order to qualify. In effect, the programs kick in when people have hit rock bottom, rather than trying to prevent them from getting there in the first place.

Parents who leave the workforce to raise their children—a job that is considered unpaid labor—could benefit from the boost of UBI.

What are the best arguments against a universal basic income?

The best argument against UBI is feasibility. You may be surprised I do not mention cost. If one multiplies the popular figure for an annual UBI—typically $12,000 a year—by the population of the United States, you get an eye-popping figure of over $3 trillion. The figure varies depending on whether children are included and at what benefit level. However, if you set this against current taxes and transfers, and conceptualize the UBI as a benefit that can be taxed for higher earners, the costs come down significantly.

The real challenge is political. First, there is significant bias against unconditional transfer programs. Most welfare programs in the United States are tied in some way to employment; for example, think of Social Security. Building popular support for a program that breaks this connection between welfare and work will require political leadership of the highest order. And then there is the enormous hurdle of integrating a UBI with the extant institutional and bureaucratic structure of the federal state. For these reasons, we may see a UBI on the state level first.

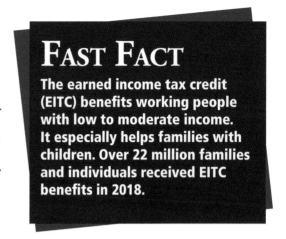

What did Milton Friedman think of the idea of a universal basic income?

Although he didn't call it a UBI, the idea of a minimum income was the earliest policy proposal Friedman came up with. In his papers, I was astounded to find his first proposal for what he called "a minimum standard of living" written in 1939. This is when he was completely unknown as an economist, although he was clearly already thinking big. Eventually, he revised it into a proposal for a negative income tax, which was enacted through the earned income tax credit, or EITC, a policy still in place today. The EITC is considered a highly successful program, with well-documented benefits for children in particular. Scholars have also found it serves to increase workforce participation among recipients.

Although he has a reputation as a radical libertarian, Friedman believed there was a clear role for the state in society. In particular, he believed there would always be persons who could not compete effectively in a market economy. He also recognized the role of luck in life, even calling the memoir he wrote with his wife, Rose, *Two Lucky People*. Whether it was temporary assistance or long-term support, Friedman saw a place for welfare. But Friedman was a great believer in the power of choice. Rather than give poor people specific benefits—food stamps, for example—he favored giving people cash that they could then bring into the marketplace and use to exercise individual choice.

Wouldn't people stop working if they got "free money"?

That's another common response to the idea of UBI. In most scenarios, the grant would not be enough to forsake paid employment altogether. The idea is that when combined with paid income, a UBI would lift the living standard of even low-skilled, low-income workers. This is why the EITC has been so effective. However, families could pool grants, perhaps enabling several members to leave the workforce altogether. This possibility has proven a point of interest both to conservatives, who point out that current welfare programs often incentivize fathers to live apart from their children, and progressives who want to provide cash benefits to mothers and others providing family care.

Milton Friedman had an interesting take on this issue. William F. Buckley asked him if he wasn't worried about people taking the money and neglecting their children, etc. Friedman responded: "If we give them the money, we will strengthen their responsibility." He seemed to be making a point that more recent social science research has fleshed out. Poverty, scholars have found, actually makes it harder to be responsible, to plan, to think about the future. When you are focused on getting enough to eat, or making rent, you don't have many psychological resources left over to focus on anything else. And, when you can't pay a traffic fine or afford safe housing, all the other foundations of a good life like steady employment and getting your children an education can also be out of reach.

What does the future hold for universal basic income in the US?

If the future of UBI can be gauged from media interest, its future is bright. Also, the idea has attracted an enormous number of high-level supporters. Particularly in Silicon Valley, it's a genuine fad, attracting adherents from entrepreneurs and tech leaders like Mark Zuckerberg and Elon Musk.

There are two challenges ahead. The first is to spread the basic idea so that it continues to move from fringe to mainstream. The second is to build it into a workable policy with a political base.

Given the fluidity of American politics right now, it could be the perfect moment for a policy that is at once utopian, bipartisan and deeply rooted in American thought.

EVALUATING THE AUTHOR'S ARGUMENTS:

In this viewpoint, interview subject Jennifer Burns suggests that UBI could build stronger families. How does she think this would happen? Do you agree? Why or why not? What are some ways UBI might affect family opportunities and interactions?

Viewpoint 2

UBI Does Not Have a Negative Effect on Work

"NIT was found to have positive effects on health and on educational metrics such as school attendance, grades, and test scores, especially amongst the most economically disadvantaged."

Wharton Public Policy Initiative

In the following viewpoint, Wharton Public Policy Initiative attempts to determine the economic effects of UBI. The authors look at groups of people who received an annual payment regardless of the amount they worked or earned. These studies found that UBI payments had, at most, a small effect on the hours people worked. At the same time, the UBI provided benefits to individuals and the economy. However, the author argues, funding a UBI program in the United States would be challenging. The Wharton Public Policy Initiative is a hub for public policy research and education from the University of Pennsylvania.

"Summary: Universal Basic Income," Wharton Public Policy Initiative.

Concern over massive structural unemployment, due to technological automation and globalization, is on the rise. Universal Basic Income (UBI) has attracted attention from both sides of the aisle as one potential solution to a scenario where a large number of people are not able to earn a livable wage. In order to understand the economic implications of UBI, economists have studied previous and current examples of UBI-type programs, analyzing their impact on consumption, labor force participation, education, health, and other key metrics.

Universal Basic Income: Background

At its core, UBI is a regular transfer of cash to all residents within a specific geographic region, for the long-term, without any conditions. UBI differs from current welfare programs in the US because it does not set an income threshold, nor does it stipulate how the money must be spent. In his 1962 book *Capitalism and Freedom*, Nobel Prize–winning economist Milton Friedman argued in favor of UBI to replace welfare programs which, he argued, disincentivized work and created welfare dependency. President Nixon was receptive to Friedman's ideas about welfare reform and, in 1971, proposed a negative income tax (NIT) transfer, a type of UBI, as the centerpiece of his welfare reform program. Nixon's reform bill was not passed by Congress and political support for UBI waned. As proposals for UBI have regained traction, a lot can be learned from earlier policy experiments during and since the Nixon administration.

Negative Income Tax (NIT) Experiments

From 1968 to 1982, the US and Canadian governments conducted five NIT experiments. Each experiment had a different guaranteed income, several with transfers of large sums of money equal to the poverty line, as well as different withdrawal rates. The effects of NIT on work showed that with a 10% increase in unearned income, the number of hours worked dropped 1%, or about 2-4 weeks over a year. The effect was not always statistically significant, however, and there were selective attrition and misreporting problems with the study's design.

Still, NIT was found to have positive effects on health and on educational metrics such as school attendance, grades, and test scores, especially amongst the most economically disadvantaged. But the implied negative impact on the overall labor force was enough leverage for opponents of UBI to diminish political interest, effectively halting the progress of UBI legislation in Congress.

Eastern Band of Cherokee Indians Casino Dividend

In 1997, the Eastern Band of Cherokees in North Carolina opened a casino on tribal land. Since then, the revenue from the casino has been given back to every tribal member, without condition, as a form of UBI. The amount of money each member receives per year averages between $4,000 and $6,000. By comparing tribal members with non-tribal members in the same area before and after 1997, economists have been able to assess the effect of the cash transfer. The data show members who receive the casino dividend work the same number of hours as those who do not, have improved education (as much as one extra year for the poorest Cherokee households), commit less crime, and have improved mental health and decreased addiction.

Alaska Permanent Fund

The Alaska Permanent Fund was created in 1976 with the stipulation that at least 25% of all revenue from the oil industry be invested and the dividends on the investment be paid out to all Alaskans, with no strings attached. Since June 1982, every Alaskan has received anywhere from $331 to $2,072 per year, depending on the performance of the investment.

The Alaska Permanent Fund provides a particularly good opportunity to study the behavioral economic impacts of UBI. The program applies to all Alaskans, whereas the other studies were not universal, and the Alaska Permanent Fund provides 30 years worth of data, making it possible to study the long-term effects. By using the synthetic control method and comparing Alaska with a composite of similar states, Professor Marienescu and co-author Damon Jones studied the causal impact of the Alaska Permanent Fund.

Evidence from the study suggests that the cash transfer Alaskans receive stimulates the local economy, with greater spending towards local businesses. The income effect, which typically leads people to work less as they receive more income, is counteracted by the increase in labor demand from industries serving the local consumers. The overall employment effect is null or slightly positive.

Lottery Winners

Winning the lottery is similar to receiving a UBI. The money is often given to the winner in installments, with no conditions, over a long duration. Furthermore, the sample is random, creating an ideal economic case study. Two such studies in the US and Sweden show consistent results: the effect of winning the lottery is similar to the effect of NIT. A 10% increase in unearned income leads to a 1% decrease in earned income. Very few people stopped working. Winning $140,000 decreases the probability of working by about 2 percentage points, with the effect being zero after 10 years. Lottery winners instead worked fewer hours but remained employed, took more vacations, and consumed more.

Financing Universal Basic Income

Is UBI financially feasible, though? There are two financing options

Studies of lottery winners give us an idea of how recipients of UBI would behave.

for UBI: (1) spending cuts to other programs, and (2) raising additional revenue. Financing will depend on the amount of the basic income. In 2017 the Organization for Economic Co-operation and Development ran a simulation of basic income for all those under 65 years of age, financed by cutting most existing types of cash benefits and tax-free allowances. The result showed that at current spending levels in the US, the non-elderly benefit per capita would fall well below the poverty line. Clearly, spending cuts would not be sufficient to fund UBI. However, if combined with additional revenue, UBI becomes more feasible in the US.

A carbon fee would be one possible source of new revenue. A recent poll showed 67% of adults in the US approved of the idea as long as it was revenue-neutral (revenue raised by the fee would not be spent by the government). The money generated by the carbon fee could finance a small UBI. This plan would incentivize a reduction in carbon pollution, help reduce negative effects on the climate, and create revenue to give a cash transfer of approximately $583 per person per year, no strings attached.

Conclusion

Based on evidence from existing studies, economists have shown giving people cash with no strings attached has only a small negative effect on work, and can improve educational and health outcomes, especially among the most disadvantaged. Paying for such a program, however, is not a trivial matter. As political appetite for UBI is growing, a new UBI program is more likely to be implemented at the state level than at the federal level.

EVALUATING THE AUTHOR'S ARGUMENTS:

This viewpoint analyzes a small number of examples where people got money without work. Can we extrapolate from these studies to assume that a UBI program would not decrease the amount people work? Why or why not? What other factors might need to be considered?

UBI Subsidizes Unpaid Work

Scott Santens

"Everyone keeps a larger percentage of the money they get for doing paid work, because of the free work unpaid workers are doing."

In the following viewpoint, Scott Santens examines the unpaid work people do. For example, many people do unpaid work caring for children and other family members. The author argues that UBI would be a Pigovian tax. This is a tax on any market activity that has a negative effect on people or society. The tax is intended to offset that effect. For example, carbon taxes charge companies for polluting the environment. The author argues that UBI would be a similar tax, helping to balance paid and unpaid work. Scott Santens is a writer and full-time advocate of unconditional basic income.

AS YOU READ, CONSIDER THE FOLLOWING QUESTIONS:
1. How much unpaid work do men and women each do on average?
2. How would UBI make up for this unpaid work, in the author's view?
3. Who benefits from this unpaid work, and how?

There's something about unpaid work that I've never actually seen discussed, and that's the cost of the work that's paid...

Take for example the amount of unpaid care work in the US that's estimated as being around $700 billion per year (and mostly done by women). That's an invisible work force comprised of 1/3 of Americans putting in over a billion hours of free work per week. What if they all went on strike and refused to work for free anymore? Perhaps because they're tired of being seen as lazy simply because the work they do isn't remunerated. Well, that work still needs to be done, right? That means the demand for paid caregivers rises considerably. Now, some of the unpaid caregivers would become paid caregivers, but they wouldn't all do that. So the price everyone pays for care work would go up due to demand exceeding supply. Additionally, government spending on care work would go up, and therefore taxes would also need to go up.

Now the interesting thing to realize here is that everyone right now is enjoying low prices and low taxes thanks to all those people

Hours Worked in One Day for Men and Women

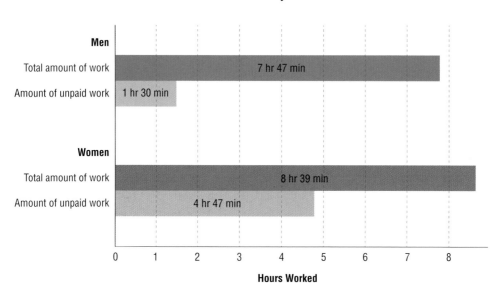

Source: Global Gender Gap Index 2016, World Economic Forum

Women bear the greatest share of unpaid labor. What would it cost to suddenly pay women for all of the work they do?

choosing to do entirely necessary work for free. Everyone's taxes are lower because of unpaid work. Everyone's prices are lower because of unpaid work. Everyone keeps a larger percentage of the money they get for doing paid work, because of the free work unpaid workers are doing.

Now consider unconditional basic income. It will go to all unpaid workers (and paid workers), and it will be paid by those being paid large enough incomes that their own basic incomes don't cover the increase in their taxes required to pay for the basic income. Remember though, unpaid work is currently lowering prices and tax burdens. So a higher tax burden is simply eliminating the artificially low tax burden, and subsidized costs.

If right now, because of unpaid work you are benefiting from invisibly, you're paying say $700 per month on care work, and it would be $1,400 per month if all unpaid workers stopped working, then you owe $700 per month to those workers. If your taxes are 30% of your income but they would be 40% if all unpaid care workers stopped working, then you owe 10% of what you earn to those workers.

Basically, just like how carbon tax is a Pigovian tax meant to correct for the unpriced negative externalities of greenhouse gas emissions, the tax increase required to fund a full basic income can be seen as Pigovian in nature too. It would be a market correcting tax where what's currently not being calculated in markets are the positive externalities of unpaid work. UBI is thus a Pigovian subsidy.

Everyone right now is benefiting from unpaid work. There is a ton of unpaid work going on. With unconditional basic income there will be even more unpaid work as that option opens up to many more people than those to whom it's currently limited—those who can afford to do unpaid work. That UBI will require an increase in taxes is simply recognizing that right now because of all the unpaid work going on, we're all receiving positive externalities without paying for them.

Complaining about higher tax rates for UBI is akin to not paying any taxes at all for roads, but driving on them every day, and enjoying the prices of goods and services that are only as low as they are because of roads, and complaining about a tax being introduced to pay for them. Paying for public roads isn't stealing. NOT paying for public roads is stealing.

One final note if it isn't obvious for those like Joe Biden. Unpaid work is work. It also tends to be more meaningful than paid work, because why else would people be doing it for free? Work that you can only get someone to do in exchange for money tends to be far less meaningful than the work people do because they simply want to do it. That should be obvious, but it unfortunately isn't because we're all just so used to money helping define one's worth.

Money does not define work's value. Wealth does not define YOUR value. Money is what we use to get people to do work they wouldn't do otherwise. If we want a world full of far more meaning, we'll automate the work people don't want to do, pay people far more for the work people don't want to do and machines don't yet make sense to do, and we'll enable everyone to pursue unpaid work over paid work.

Unconditional basic income is the foundation of that new world.

EVALUATING THE AUTHOR'S ARGUMENTS:

Viewpoint author Scott Santens claims that UBI is a way to pay people for care work they're already doing. Therefore, higher taxes are simply paying money we already owe. Do you agree with his conclusions that UBI is similar to paying taxes to support the roads people use? Why or why not?

Working for Money Is Overrated

Anna Dent

"The notion that paid employment is the cure to all ills has been seriously undermined."

In the following viewpoint, Anna Dent debates the value of paid work. She argues that low-paid workers struggle to ever improve their jobs or their lives. Once established, economic inequalities tend to continue. If UBI provided enough money for people to survive without work, they could spend their time on other options, such as starting new businesses, caring for family members, being creative, or volunteering. Anna Dent is a freelance policy and research consultant. She covers topics such as employment, skills, and welfare.

AS YOU READ, CONSIDER THE FOLLOWING QUESTIONS:
1. How does work add and remove value in people's lives?
2. What additional options would people have if UBI allowed them to turn down work?
3. If UBI is instituted, is it likely to allow people to opt out of work entirely?

T he danger of so-called "free money" not only underpins critiques of universal basic income (UBI), but also the incredibly strong narratives that underlie the attitudes to work in the UK (and elsewhere)—and our unemployment benefit system. Paid employment is held up as one of the ultimate markers of being a valuable member of society, with those not in paid work (always described in these narratives as a voluntary position, rather than as the result of issues outside their control) seen as a drain on society. Those out of work are positioned in direct contrast to those in paid employment: the shirkers versus the strivers, the "welfare dependent" versus the hardworking families.

For those in paid work, working hard and being constantly busy are worn as a badge of pride, and there are whole industries promising to make us more productive and efficient. For some, hard work is enforced through workplace monitoring, impossibly short breaks or expectations of staff being "always on," for example responding to emails outside work hours. Work is idealised as providing meaning in our lives, while at the same time removing us from other sources of meaning, such as family, friends and our communities, through long hours and unpaid overtime. The negative psychological, social and physical effects of these narratives and assumptions are now being investigated, and the centrality of work in our lives and society questioned.

Preliminary results from Finland's basic income experiment found little to no impact on recipients' likelihood of undertaking paid employment. This has led some to suggest that the experiment is a failure—indeed, the Finnish government had hoped the plan would increase participation in paid work. However, although it was not a trial of a full UBI (universal, unconditional, non-withdrawable and non means-tested) it is being celebrated by many who advocate the idea, as it provides important evidence about the interaction of UBI and work. One of the major objections is that getting "free money" would undermine recipients' motivation to undertake paid work: the Finnish case shows this is not so.

The notion that paid employment is the cure to all ills has been seriously undermined, if it were ever true. Work as the best route out of poverty may still hold true for some, but the majority of

Many people with full-time jobs can't earn a living because of low wages.

households in poverty in the UK are now consistently those with at least one person in work. The likelihood of people becoming stuck in low-wage, low-skilled work is significant, and hard work among the lower paid is doing nothing to reduce economic inequalities. Coupled with the potential threat to many jobs and industries from automation and AI (although we need to be careful not to overstate this), the relentless prioritisation of paid work seems less defensible.

Whether we derive meaning from employment, or find ourselves engaged in meaningless "bull*** jobs" as David Graeber suggests, we cannot deny that the world of work is changing. Climate change, mass migration and continued technological change will all have impacts on what "work" means and looks like in ways that we cannot accurately predict.

For its proponents, a UBI can provide a lifejacket and a route through some of these challenges. A UBI could provide a stable

FAST FACT

Millions of full-time workers earn wages that put them below the poverty line in the US. Over half of these workers are people of color.

income floor, a guaranteed minimum below which no one would fall. Depending on the amount paid, it could enable low-paid workers to turn down the worst jobs on offer, or enable time away from paid work to retrain, or start a business. It would financially compensate those (usually women) caring for family for their work, support more people to be creative, to volunteer, or simply to do nothing. In the US, proposals for a Green New Deal led by Democrats Alexandria Ocasio-Cortez and Ed Markey appear to advocate for something like a UBI—potentially for those "unwilling" to work, although it is light on detail.

A UBI is not designed to promote "laziness" or any other type of behaviour, simply to allow individuals to make their own decisions about how they wish to spend their time. The pure idea of a UBI does not hold any inherent position when it comes to paid work, but promises freedom and choice. As far back as the 1880s, in the work of Paul Lafargue, the right of workers (as opposed to the rich) to be lazy was framed as an explicit rejection of the dominant work ethic, and the route to true independence, free from the pressure to work. The refusal to participate in paid employment is still considered by some as an active strategy of resistance to neoliberalism. A UBI as a way to live securely without paid employment features regularly in mainly leftwing discussions about post-work, interrogating the centrality of paid employment in our lives and societies, and our ability to liberate ourselves, or be liberated from, our roles as paid workers.

In reality, the likelihood of any western country introducing a UBI at a rate to enable the average worker to entirely opt out of paid employment is extremely low (in Finland, participants received €560 (£475) a month, in Ontario, participants were guaranteed a minimum income of $16,989 (£13,185) a year). Most of the current trials around the world actively frame UBI as a pro-employment policy, smoothing the sharp edges of benefit systems and the insecurities of the modern labour market, to make paid employment more feasible, attractive and sustainable. The utopian vision of a life of leisure in which a UBI offers us a comfortable standard of living is not about to become reality, but the ideas of working less, and receiving a stable, humane basic income are gaining traction and starting to influence debate in ways unthinkable even 10 years ago.

EVALUATING THE AUTHOR'S ARGUMENTS:

Viewpoint author Anna Dent questions society's tendency to hold up working for pay as an ideal value. What kinds of people don't work for pay? Come up with as many examples as you can. Why don't they work for pay? Is that good, bad, or neither?

American Opinions Are Split on UBI

Edward Freeland

"Being primed to think about nonprofit sponsored aid in Africa makes one more inclined to support government sponsored UBI in the US."

In the following viewpoint, Edward Freeland considers American attitudes toward UBI. A study asked Americans about their support for UBI in the United States, as well as their support for UBI as charitable aid to Africa. The study found that people are roughly divided in their support or opposition to UBI. Differences exist based on sex, race, age, and education. The researchers also found that asking the questions in different orders affected the results. Edward Freeland is the associate director of the Princeton Survey Research Center at Princeton University.

AS YOU READ, CONSIDER THE FOLLOWING QUESTIONS:
1. Are women or men more likely to support UBI?
2. How do factors such as race and age affect support for UBI?
3. How did the order of the questions affect support for UBI?

"What Do Americans Think About Universal Basic Income?" by Edward Freeland, USC Evidence Base Blog, August 26, 2019. Reprinted by permission.

Most people agree that society has a responsibility to meet the basic needs of its children.

The concept of a Universal Basic Income (UBI) is turning up more often these days in debates over income inequality, poverty and the impact of automation on the labor force. It's an old idea that traces back to Sir Thomas More's *Utopia* and appears later in the writings of social philosophers such as Condorcet, Thomas Paine, Charles Fourier, and John Stuart Mills. In the 1960s, economist Milton Friedman proposed a "negative income tax" that would replace America's patchwork system of social welfare programs with unconditional cash payments that would be enough to cover the basic costs of food and shelter for low income households. Friedman's idea was the basis for the Family Assistance Program that was proposed (and then defeated) during the Nixon Administration. Recently the idea has drawn renewed interest because of skepticism about the effectiveness of aid programs in developing nations and concerns about workers who will be displaced in the near future by robots and artificial intelligence. Several countries around the world and several cities in the US have announced their interest in UBI, and some have launched experiments designed to test its feasibility.

For the most part, public opinion on the subject of UBI has been divided. A 2017 poll by Gallup found a near even split among American adults between those who support UBI (48%) and those who do not (52%). A Zogby Strategies poll done around the same time found 40% in favor of UBI, 35% opposed, and 25% undecided. A 2017 international survey by IPSOS found a more even split among Americans, with 38% in favor, 38% opposed and 24% undecided. Among other nations in the poll, support for UBI was found to be lowest in countries such as France (29%) and Spain (31%) and highest in Poland (60%) and Germany (52%). Switzerland is the only country that has had a national referendum on this issue. In 2016, voters there rejected a proposal to give each person a monthly cash allowance of 2,500 Swiss francs (about $2,000 US dollars when you factor in the cost of living) by a margin of nearly 3 to 1.

We added four questions to the January/February 2019 Understanding America Study omnibus survey to get an update on opinions of UBI from a representative sample of American adults (UAS 167). We had four objectives:

- Gauge current public support for government sponsored UBI in the US
- Measure support for UBI programs sponsored by nonprofit organizations for people living in the poorest parts of Africa
- Measure how much people agree on society's obligation to provide for the basic needs of all children regardless of where they are born
- Test the effect of asking about government sponsored UBI in the US conditional on having first thought about nonprofit sponsored UBI in the poorest parts of Africa

Here are the questions (the order of questions 1 and 2 was randomized):

1. Some business executives have proposed that the US government should provide every American with a Universal Basic Income, that is, a minimum amount of money each month so they can afford a basic level of shelter, healthcare and food. Do you support or oppose this idea?
   1. Support
   2. Oppose
   3. No Opinion

2. Some charities and international aid organizations have proposed using their funds to provide people living in the poorest parts of Africa with a Universal Basic Income, that is, a minimum amount of money each month so they can afford a basic level of shelter, healthcare and food. Do you support or oppose this idea?
   1. Support
   2. Oppose
   3. No Opinion

3. To what extent do you agree or disagree with the following statement:
All children, no matter where they are born, should be provided the opportunity to go to school, develop their talents, live safely and receive medical care when they need it.
   1. Agree strongly
   2. Agree somewhat
   3. Neither agree nor disagree
   4. Disagree somewhat
   5. Disagree strongly

In terms of public support for government sponsored UBI in the US, our results are in line with those found in previous polls: 37% support it, 40% are opposed and 23% have no opinion. Women are more likely to be UBI supporters than men (40% support vs. 35% support), people with bachelor's degrees are more likely to be opposed to UBI than those with less education (46% opposed vs. 37% opposed); non-Hispanic whites are also less likely to support UBI than everyone else in the sample (31% support vs. 52% support). People below the median age for the sample (53 years) are more likely to support UBI than those who are older (41% support vs. 33% support). People with household incomes below the median are also more likely to be domestic UBI supporters.

On the question of non-profit funded UBI for people living in the poorest parts of Africa, support among adults in the US is somewhat stronger, although a higher proportion have no opinion: 41% support it, 25% are opposed and 34% have no opinion. When we look at the demographic differences explored above in question 1, we find similar patterns of support and opposition, although there is a big drop (23 percentage points) in opposition among the more highly educated, with 9% of people with bachelor's degrees moving from opposing UBI in the US to supporting UBI in Africa and 14% moving from opposing UBI in the US to no opinion on UBI in Africa.

As noted earlier, we randomized the order of appearance for questions 1 and 2. Our null hypothesis was that the randomization would make no difference in whether one supports or opposes either type of UBI. However, we find that responses to both questions are indeed impacted by their order of appearance.

When the question about government-sponsored UBI in the US appears first, support for nonprofit-sponsored UBI in Africa decreases by seven percentage points (from 44% to 37%). This shift is consistent across all race/ethnic groups in the sample and appears to be unrelated to any differences in education, age or sex. Irrespective of demographic differences, being asked first about government-sponsored UBI in the US appears to make one less sympathetic to the idea of nonprofit-sponsored UBI for poor Africans.

Why this outcome? It's possible that respondents misunderstood (or ignored) the difference in the source of funding for the two different forms of UBI. Perhaps government-sponsored UBI in the US was perceived as a domestic aid program and nonprofit-sponsored UBI in Africa was perceived as a foreign aid program. We know from other polls (e.g., the GSS) that while neither form of assistance is popular, spending on foreign aid is much less popular than spending on domestic welfare programs. So, it's possible that the difference in geography loomed larger in the minds of respondents than the difference in funding sources.

But what happens when we ask first about support for government-sponsored UBI in the US? If we ask respondents first about this type of UBI, 33% say they support it. But when we ask first about nonprofit-sponsored UBI in Africa, support for government-sponsored UBI in the US rises to 42%, an increase of 9 percentage points. Thus, it appears that being primed to think about nonprofit sponsored aid in Africa makes one more inclined to support government sponsored UBI in the US. Here again, the difference in geography may have been more cognitively salient to respondents than the difference in the funding sources.

These two ordering effects (the negative effect for Africa when we ask first about UBI in the US and the positive effect for the US when we ask about UBI in Africa first) hold up even in multivariate logistic regressions of support for the two forms of UBI on a set of demographic factors where we include the order of appearance as a predictor variable.

As for our third question, the one about whether all children, regardless of where they are born, should have their basic needs met, 66 percent of respondents strongly agreed and another 20 percent agreed somewhat. Only eight percent said they neither agreed nor disagreed. Here we find a significant decrease in the percent of respondents offering a "don't know" response. In addition, responses to this question are not significantly impacted by the order of appearance of the first two questions.

In sum, we find that our results are very much in line with the results of previous polls and surveys: support for and opposition to Universal Basic Income are roughly equivalent with a significant percentage of the sample offering a "don't know" response. If, in the near future, the issue of UBI starts to gain political traction, public opinion researchers should be mindful of the apparent ease with which responses can be pushed in one direction or another by the order in which questions are presented. While support for UBI is likely to remain counterbalanced by opposition, advocates can take some solace in the strong support found among most Americans for the general principle that all kids, no matter where they are born, should have their basic needs met by the larger society.

EVALUATING THE AUTHOR'S ARGUMENTS:

The primary survey Edward Freeland refers to in this viewpoint asked people about their opinions on UBI in the United States and about aid to Africa. Do you think it's fair to equate these two things? How does considering them together affect people's responses? Why might that be? What does this tell us about the potential accuracy of opinion surveys?

Chapter 3

How Could We Pay for UBI?

The money to fund UBI has to come from somewhere, of course. But where?

Know the Numbers Required by UBI

"It is very unlikely that the UBI would be able to produce significant growth on a persistent basis."

Kyle Pomerleau

In the following viewpoint, Kyle Pomerleau considers a 2019 proposal by then presidential candidate Andrew Yang that would have provided Americans with a UBI. The author argues that the plan would not have been financially feasible. One area of contention is whether implementing a UBI would cause economic growth. While Yang believed it would, this author doubts the growth would be significant and long-lasting. He argues that the plan would need to be changed in order to pay for itself. Kyle Pomerleau is a resident fellow at the American Enterprise Institute (AEI), where he studies federal tax policy.

AS YOU READ, CONSIDER THE FOLLOWING QUESTIONS:
1. What did Andrew Yang's plan hope to do?
2. How would the plan have paid for UBI?
3. Does this author believe UBI is possible under different circumstances?

"Does Andrew Yang's 'Freedom Dividend' Proposal Add Up?" by Kyle Pomerleau, Tax Foundation, July 24, 2019. https://taxfoundation.org/andrew-yang-value-added-tax-universal-basic-income/. Licensed under CC BY-NC 4.0.

D uring the first Democratic presidential debates, Andrew Yang said he wants to provide each American adult $1,000 per month in a universal basic income (UBI) he calls a "Freedom Dividend." He argued that this proposal could be paid for with a value-added tax at half the rate levied by European countries.

Many people, including myself, expressed skepticism that a 10 percent value-added tax (VAT) could fund a cash transfer this large. According to his website, however, there is more to the plan than a VAT. He argues that he could fund his Freedom Dividend with a combination of new revenue from a VAT, other taxes, spending cuts, and economic growth.

But even accounting for revenue from other sources and potentially lower government spending on current transfer payments, it's very unlikely that his plan adds up.

We estimate that his plan, as described, could only fund a little less than half the Freedom Dividend at $1,000 a month.

A more realistic plan would require reducing the Freedom Dividend to $750 per month and raising the VAT to 22 percent.

Details of Yang's Freedom Dividend

Yang's proposal is to provide $1,000 per month ($12,000 a year) to each adult citizen. A core feature of the Freedom Dividend is that individuals would need to choose between their current government benefits and the Freedom Dividend. As such, some individuals may decline the Freedom Dividend if they determine that their current government benefits are more valuable.

The benefits that individuals would need to give up are Supplemental Nutritional Assistance Program (SNAP), Temporary Assistance for Needed Families (TANF), Supplemental Security Income (SSI), and SNAP for Women, Infants, and Child Program (WIC).

To cover the additional cost of the Freedom Dividend, Yang would raise revenue in five ways:
- A 10 percent VAT
- A tax on financial transactions
- Taxing capital gains and carried interest at ordinary income rates

Presidential candidate Andrew Yang drew attention and plenty of support with his plan for a universal basic income program.

- Remove the wage cap on the Social Security payroll tax
- A $40 per metric ton carbon tax

The Budgetary Effect of the Freedom Dividend Plan

Calculating the gross cost of the Freedom Dividend is straightforward. According to an analysis of Yang's Freedom Dividend by the UBI Center, an open source think tank researching universal basic income policies, there are about 236 million adult citizens in the United States. At $12,000 a piece, the total gross cost of the dividend would be $2.8 trillion each year.

Using the Tax Foundation model, we estimate that the five tax increases in his plan would raise $1.3 trillion each year on a conventional basis. Most of the revenue would come from the VAT. We estimate that a 10 percent VAT with a very broad base (about 66 percent of GDP) would raise $952 billion each year. Removing the cap on the Social Security payroll tax would raise an additional $133 billion. A carbon tax at $40 per metric ton would raise an additional $123 billion. A financial transactions tax would raise about $78 billion. Finally, taxing capital gains and dividends at ordinary income rates would raise $7 billion each year.

In addition to revenue from taxes, Yang would rely on two additional offsets to pay for the Freedom Dividend. First, the federal government would save money from individuals who decline the cash transfer in favor of their current benefits and from those who give up their current benefits if they opt for the cash benefit. According to the UBI Center, this effect is expected to offset $151 billion each year.

Second, Yang also argues that his Freedom Dividend would produce economic growth. This economic growth would broaden the existing tax base as individuals would earn more income. His website says that he expects between $800 billion and $900 billion per year in additional revenue from economic growth.

Annual Budgetary Effect of Andrew Yang's Tax Proposals and Freedom Dividend (Negative Number = Increase in Deficit)

Proposal	Annual Revenue (Billions of 2019 Dollars)
Cost of the Freedom Dividend	-$2,800
10 Percent Value-Added Tax	$952
Financial Transactions Tax	$78
Tax Capital Gains at Ordinary Income Tax Rates	$7
Remove the Cap on Social Security Payroll Tax	$129
Carbon Tax ($40 per Metric Ton)	$124
Total Tax Revenue	$1,291
Offset from Reduced Federal Spending/Welfare Overlap	$151
Offset from Reduced Economic Activity	-$124
Total Effect of Non-Tax Offsets	$27
Net Effect	-$1,482

Source: Tax Foundation General Equilibrium Model, April 2019; Congressional Budget Office; and UBI Center Analysis.

Annual Budgetary Effect of a Budget-Neutral Version of the Freedom Dividend (Negative Number = Increase in Deficit)

Proposal	Annual Revenue (Billions of 2019 Dollars)
Cost of the Freedom Dividend	-$2,100
22 Percent Value-Added Tax	$1,904
Financial Transactions Tax	$71
Tax Capital Gains at Ordinary Income Tax Rates	$7
Remove the Cap on Social Security Payroll Tax	$112
Carbon Tax ($40 per Metric Ton)	$124
Total Tax Revenue	$2,218
Offset from Reduced Federal Spending/Welfare Overlap	$144
Offset from Reduced Economic Activity	-$275
Total Effect of Non-Tax Offsets	-$131
Net Effect (Negative = Increase in Deficit)	-$13

Source: Tax Foundation General Equilibrium Model, April 2019; Congressional Budget Office; and UBI Center Analysis.

While it is possible that the UBI could produce a short-term increase in economic activity, it is very unlikely that it would be able to produce significant growth on a persistent basis.

It is more likely that his overall plan would reduce the long-run size of the economy and the tax base. The three major taxes in his plan (VAT, carbon tax, and payroll tax increase), while efficient sources of revenue, would tend to reduce labor force participation by reducing the after-tax returns to working.

Using the Tax Foundation Model, we estimate that the weighted average marginal tax rate on labor income would increase by about 8.6 percentage points. The resulting reduction in hours worked would ultimately reduce output by 3 percent. We estimate that Yang would lose about $124 billion each year in revenue due to the lower output.

Overall, we estimate that his proposal to provide a $12,000 unconditional cash transfer, paid for by tax increases and slightly lower federal spending on other programs, would end up increasing the budget deficit by about $1.5 trillion each year even after accounting for offsetting reductions in government spending and changes in economic output.

A Revenue-Neutral Freedom Dividend

To make Yang's Freedom Dividend revenue-neutral, he either needs to propose higher taxes or provide a smaller unconditional cash transfer.

One possible way to make the plan sustainable would be to raise the VAT. But to make sure the VAT doesn't go far higher than the global norm, Yang could also reduce the generosity of the cash payment.

We estimate that a revenue-neutral version of the Freedom Dividend would reduce the value of the cash benefit by 25 percent ($9,000 per year instead of $12,000) and would need a broad-based VAT of 22 percent.

To make things simple, we assume that reducing the size of the cash benefit by 25 percent would reduce its cost in proportion. As such a $9,000 annual benefit would cost $2.1 trillion.

On the revenue side, we estimate that a 22 percent VAT would be sufficient to fund a $9,000 UBI. Increasing the VAT does a few things. First, the tax itself raises significantly more revenue ($1.9 trillion up from $952 billion). Second, the VAT reduces the potential revenue effects of the other tax proposals. This is because the VAT mechanically reduces the income and payroll tax base by reducing payments made to workers and owners of capital. Lastly, more than doubling the VAT increases the marginal tax rate on labor, increasing the negative offset from the smaller economy.

In addition, the reduced generosity of the cash transfer would mean that more people would opt to stay on current government benefits. According to the UBI Center, the offset would be $144 billion each year under a $9,000 per year UBI.

Conclusion

Andrew Yang's central proposal for his campaign is a universal basic income (UBI) called the "Freedom Dividend." His current proposal to offer a $12,000 cash transfer to each US adult citizen would cost about $2.8 trillion each year. He would rely on several new taxes, including a 10 percent value-added tax (VAT), and other non-tax offsets to fund this proposal. We estimate that overall, his taxes and offsets would not be enough to cover the cost of his Freedom Dividend. We estimate that one option to make his proposal sustainable would be to raise the VAT rate to 22 percent and reduce the cash transfer to $9,000 per year.

Modeling Notes

Unless otherwise noted, the estimates are produced using the Tax Foundation's General Equilibrium Model. The model can produce both conventional and dynamic revenue estimates of tax policy. Conventional estimates hold the size of the economy constant and attempts to estimate potential behavioral effects of tax policy. Dynamic revenue estimates consider both behavioral and macroeconomic effects of tax policy on revenue. The model can also produce estimates of how policies impact measures of economic performance such as GDP, wages, employment, the capital stock, investment, consumption, saving, and the trade deficit. Lastly, it can produce estimates of how different tax policy impacts the distribution of the federal tax burden.

In modeling the VAT, we assumed a broad base that applies to all goods and services and a noncompliance rate of 15 percent, roughly the average compliance rate for the overall US tax system. Higher levels on noncompliance would ultimately result in less revenue from the VAT.

Yang's website specifies that he would enact a 0.1 percent financial transactions tax. However, it does not specify the base on which this tax would be levied.

We assumed that the proposal would roughly match the option modeled by the CBO in its Options publication.

We assumed that Yang would enact a carbon tax at the same rate proposed by the Climate Leadership Council at $40 per metric ton.

The CLC proposal would recycle the revenue into a "carbon dividend" similar to Yang's. We assume that there would be no separate carbon dividend and that all the revenue would be used to fund the Freedom Dividend.

To simplify the analysis, we assumed that changes in economic output do not affect government spending.

EVALUATING THE AUTHOR'S ARGUMENTS:

Viewpoint author Kyle Pomerleau is a tax expert who argues with the numbers proposed in one UBI plan. How can people judge whether or not a plan's finances will work out as promised? Why might experts come up with different numbers? If experts disagree, whom should we believe?

Viewpoint 2

Universal Basic Income Alone Isn't the Answer

ATD Fourth World

"If we really want to fight poverty, we cannot only talk about income."

In the following viewpoint, ATD Fourth World describes a panel discussion at the United Nations. The panel reviewed studies of how people living in poverty felt about UBI. While people in poverty saw many advantages, they were not all confident that UBI was the best answer to their problems. They worried that it would not help them get jobs and find productive places in society. The viewpoint argues that UBI may help end extreme poverty, but other programs will also be necessary. ATD Fourth World is a nonprofit organization trying to end chronic poverty.

AS YOU READ, CONSIDER THE FOLLOWING QUESTIONS:
1. Why are many people uncomfortable applying for welfare aid?
2. How can extreme poverty cause people to feel shame?
3. Do people living in poverty want to work or not, in general?

"A Universal Basic Income: The Solution to Ending Extreme Poverty?" ATD Fourth World, July 11, 2017. Reprinted by permission.

Would providing everyone with a guaranteed income end the problem of homelessness?

On June 8, 2017, ATD Fourth World organized a panel discussion at the UN with Philip Alston, the Special Rapporteur on Extreme Poverty and Human Rights on the subject of a universal basic income. Thirteen governments from all regions, three UN agencies and over 50 NGOs attended the event. Isabelle Doresse, the person responsible for ATD People's Universities in the north of France, talked about the reactions of people living in extreme poverty to the idea of a universal basic income. Surprisingly, there were a number of hesitations and concerns about the idea.

Background

The idea of providing a basic income to every member of society is one that has been gaining ground over the last years—even in Silicon Valley! It would be "basic" because everyone in a society would receive a monthly income that would provide a "floor" to help meet basic needs. And it would be "universal" because everyone would receive it, regardless of their level of income. The idea is seen as a solution to many of today's concerns. It would help to reduce the growing disparities and it would ensure a level of financial security. In addition, it would make better use of available funds because it would eliminate the bureaucracy currently in place to implement welfare programmes. Finally, it would provide an income to people (often women) who spend much of their lives in care-giving.

The idea has gained enough ground that it was discussed in the recent French presidential campaign. And so ATD France wanted to know what people living in extreme poverty thought about the idea—after all, they were one of the main groups of beneficiaries that people had in mind.

Four meetings of ATD's People's University programme in France worked on the topic. In addition, a European Fourth World People's University took place in December 2016, where participants from Belgium, France, Ireland, Netherlands, and Spain worked on a guaranteed right to the means necessary to live decently.

Interestingly, the reaction was not wild enthusiasm. The idea was welcomed as providing some clear advantages, but also some dangers.

What Did People See as the Advantages?

First, perhaps a universal basic income would reduce stigmatization. As expressed over and over again by the people with whom ATD Fourth World works in France, when you are on welfare, you are suspected of not wanting to work, of liking to live off of others, of cheating by hiding income or by lying about the family's situation.

Receiving a basic income is not perceived as a right, but as a humiliating aid. So 35% of people who are eligible to be on welfare don't request it, because of the lack of information and the complexity of the procedures, but also because the procedures are too intrusive and too constraining. One person said: "There are lots of indiscreet questions, when you establish a welfare file. I didn't want to answer, but you have to talk about your private life, if you want to be helped."

Second, universal minimum income should allow everyone to live in dignity and to have access to basic necessities; they would not be forced to make impossible choices. Extreme poverty is not only a problem of material deprivation. As stated in the UN Guiding Principles on Extreme Poverty and Human Rights: extreme poverty is the result of insecurity in several areas of life, that is persistent, and that compromises the chances for people to reclaim their rights by themselves. Extreme poverty gives people a feeling of failure and shame, and so affects their self-confidence and self-esteem.

As one participant said, "If we constantly are running out of money, if we are in a constant state of anxiety about how we are going to make ends meet and raise our children, then we can't live in dignity."

Third, a basic minimum income can help empower people, for it would no longer keep them in a position of dependence and insecurity.

One person said: "I go from shelter to shelter. There's no stability. I can't plan for tomorrow. It makes me feel very insecure."

A mother stated: "The social worker tells me to pay my rent first, but I can't. My first choice is my daughter's education. I pay for school and music first."

Fourth, people would no longer be maintained beneath the poverty line, since the current system discourages initiatives to increase their incomes.

As one man in the People's University explained: "During the summer holidays, my daughter had a job. When the holidays ended, she went back to the social service center to pick up the family allowance but was told she was not eligible for it because she was working, even though she provided papers proving she was no longer working. She is struggling more than before."

Another participant provided this example: "A girl obtained a scholarship for her studies but this scholarship was then deducted from her mother's minimum income. It was like she had no scholarship anymore…"

A universal basic income could provide a floor on which a person can build through his or her work, however minimal that amount is. Similarly, if the person loses their income from work, a basic income could maintain his or her rights without delay and without difficulty. This means that the basic income should be allocated to each individual person, and not calculated by household.

People in Poverty See Risks

Serious concerns were expressed about the idea in the People's University discussions. People living in poverty would prefer to be able to live from their work. With a universal basic income, they are afraid of being permanently excluded from the world of work, to which they aspire. They are afraid they would be told, "Now, with the basic income, you have some money, we don't want to hear from you anymore."

A basic income would provide an income, but it does not allow for insertion into society, the recognition, the self-realization that people seek.

Also, the minimum income policy must be integrated into a comprehensive policy to eradicate extreme poverty. If we really want to fight poverty, we cannot only talk about income. The policy for the right "to an adequate means of subsistence" must be closely coordinated with policies for access to decent housing, to health care, to education, to employment… Other forms of family support would need to be maintained.

And the policies to fight extreme poverty must be designed, implemented and evaluated with the concerned people. Experiments with a universal basic income or other anti-poverty approaches should involve people living in poverty from the outset. Only then will we succeed in eradicating extreme poverty.

EVALUATING THE AUTHOR'S ARGUMENTS:

Viewpoint author ATD Fourth World argues that while UBI has many advantages to people in poverty, it is not the end of their problems. People want to work and have a place in society. Do you think UBI would help or hinder that process? If you wanted to implement UBI, what other factors would you consider?

UBI Is, First and Foremost, Tax Policy

Alexander Holt

"UBI isn't really about welfare spending: It's about tax policy."

In the following viewpoint, Alexander Holt references an article from the *New York Times* that claimed UBI would hurt the poor. The author challenges those claims and says that if UBI is seen as a new US tax policy, it ultimately could help the rich more than the poor. UBI would create a more progressive system that would reduce the tax breaks wealthy people now get. Alexander Holt is a writer and computer scientist. New America is a think tank in Washington, DC, that focuses on public policy issues including the economy.

AS YOU READ, CONSIDER THE FOLLOWING QUESTIONS:

1. Who saves the most money under the current tax system in the United States?
2. Would wealthy people pay more or less in taxes under the program the author outlines?
3. Is this author suggesting that welfare programs should be cut as UBI is started?

"Universal Income Is About Taxes, Not Spending," by Alexander Holt, New America, June 2, 2016. https://www.newamerica.org/weekly/universal-income-about-taxes-not-spending/. Licensed under CC BY 4.0.

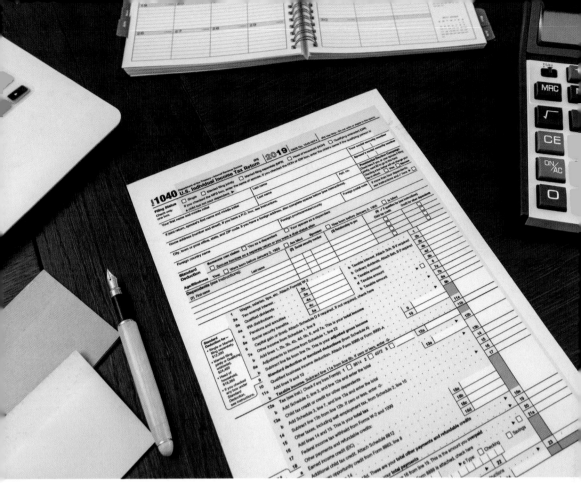

Should UBI be funded through tax expenditures?

Universal Basic Income (UBI), a policy in which every American would receive a set amount of cash each year from the government, suddenly has a lot of lovers and haters. Eduardo Porter is a hater. In the *New York Times* this Tuesday, he warned readers that UBI is a bad idea that would hurt the poor. He said UBI is too expensive, and that the only way to pay for it would be through massive tax increases and eliminating social welfare programs. This would be a sound argument if it didn't miss the point. UBI isn't really about welfare spending: It's about tax policy.

UBI is an unconditional cash transfer, which means you get money from the government to spend however you want. That's an unusual government spending program—besides social security, the government usually either spends money on a service (like healthcare or education) or gives conditional cash in the form of things like food stamps. But the government also spends a lot of money each year on cash transfers through "tax expenditures," which is the money the government doesn't collect in taxes due to exclusions in the tax code. Except for the Earned Income Tax Credit, those expenditures almost always help the rich more than the poor. By replacing them with UBI, we would create a more progressive system. That, not the elimination of all government programs, should be the starting place for debates about UBI.

When people file taxes, most claim a "standard deduction" and "personal exemption," two policies that combine to subtract about $10,000 from your taxable income. If you make over $38,000 in a single household, you save about $2,500 a year on your taxes, because your marginal tax rate is 25 percent (in this case, 25 percent times $10,000). If you make over $415,000, it's worth $3,960 a year, because your tax rate is 39.6 percent. So, the higher your tax bracket, the more the deductions are worth.

What's more, the richest 20 percent of Americans form the vast majority of those who deduct even more than $10,000 because of their ability to "itemize" deductions. Although only one-third of tax filers itemize, they deduct a lot. That's because they pay more in state and local taxes, have more expensive houses (and therefore more mortgage interest), and give a lot to nonprofits.

A 2013 report by the nonpartisan Congressional Budget Office said that the richest 20 percent of Americans make up 81 percent of the value for the three biggest itemized deductions (state and local taxes, mortgage interest, and charitable giving). That same report said that the benefits of those deductions "equal less than 0.1 percent of after-tax income for the lowest income quintile, 0.4 percent for the middle quintile, 2.5 percent for the highest quintile, and 3.9 percent for the top percentile." The three of them cost a combined $185 billion a year.

And while many would oppose eliminating the charitable and mortgage interest deductions—it would be more expensive for rich Americans to put their names on college buildings and pay off the mortgage on their expensive houses—many Americans will receive cash from the government each month that they can choose to donate to charities. Since the majority of Americans do not use the charitable deduction, UBI could even encourage more donations throughout the year.

So, if tomorrow we gave everyone $2,500 a year through UBI but eliminated the standard deduction, personal exemption, and itemized deductions, most people earning above $37,000 wouldn't receive any new money, and those earning above $91,000 would actually lose money.

But that's not all. If UBI were considered regular income, wealthy people lose even more money compared to the current system. Consider again the $2,500 example. Since the richest face a 39.6 percent marginal tax rate, they would actually only get $1,510 from the government after taxes. In the past, had they claimed the standard deduction and personal exemption and had there been no UBI, they would have gotten about $3,960.

UBI does not necessarily mean more free money for everyone. To pay for even this modest program, we may need to raise some new taxes even after ridding the tax code of deductions. And to be clear, eliminating deductions and exemptions is a tax increase on wealthier individuals. They would have to pay more than they do now and would get less money. But lower income Americans would get more.

Advocates of UBI talk about $10,000 or $20,000 annual cash transfers. But UBI itself just means giving people some sum of money—there's nothing that says it has to be extremely expensive at the start. The case described above is about the relatively limited amount of $2,500. And the beauty of it being universal is that it could have broad political support, just like the current standard deduction and personal exemption have now. The difference is that, while those deductions and exemptions are regressive and popular, UBI would be progressive and popular.

Over time, perhaps, there could be political support for increasing UBI above $2,500. Maybe as it increases, fewer social welfare programs would be needed and therefore eliminated. But it would be a slow process. UBI would first be, and indeed is, tax policy, and all of us—even the haters—ought to treat it that way.

EVALUATING THE AUTHOR'S ARGUMENTS:

Viewpoint author Alexander Holt suggests starting with a low UBI, such as $2,500 per year, in order to build support for the concept and see how it plays out. Do you think it makes sense to start with an amount such as this? Or should people commit to funding a UBI that would fully support people, or skip UBI altogether? Why?

VAT and UBI Could Work Together

William G. Gale

"If new revenues are an inevitable part of any effort to control the federal budget, a VAT with a UBI could be one of the best policy options."

In the following viewpoint, William G. Gale describes a plan to implement UBI in the US along with a VAT. In this plan, a family of four would receive about $5,200 per year. This amount would not be nearly enough to support the family, but it would offset the extra costs of the VAT and provide some additional resources. The author argues that both liberals and conservatives should be able to support this plan, as it could control the federal budget while helping people in poverty. William G. Gale is the former vice president and director of the Economic Studies Program at the Brookings Institution.

AS YOU READ, CONSIDER THE FOLLOWING QUESTIONS:
1. How much money would a 10% VAT raise and in what time frame?
2. How would this policy affect people in different income brackets?
3. Why does the author believe people across the political spectrum should agree to this plan?

"How a VAT Could Tax the Rich and Pay for Universal Basic Income," by William G. Gale, The Brookings Institution, January 30, 2020. Reprinted by permission.

The Congressional Budget Office just projected a series of $1 trillion budget deficits—as far as the eye can see. Narrowing that deficit will require not only spending reductions and economic growth but also new taxes. One solution that I've laid out in a new Hamilton Project paper, "Raising Revenue with a Progressive Value-Added Tax," is a 10 percent Value-Added Tax (VAT) combined with a universal basic income (UBI)—effectively a cash payment to every US household.

The plan would raise substantial net revenue, be very progressive, and be as conducive to economic growth as any other new tax. The VAT would complement, not replace, any new direct taxes on affluent households, such as a wealth tax or capital gains reforms.

A VAT is a national consumption tax—like a retail sales tax but collected in small bits at each stage of production. It raises a lot of revenue without distorting economic choices like saving, investment, or the organizational form of businesses. And it can be easier to administer than retail sales taxes.

An American VAT

The structure of an American VAT should mirror those of the most effective existing VATs around the world. It should be built on a broad consumption base. It should adjust (impose or rebate) taxes at the border so it applies only to goods and services purchased in the US no matter where they are produced. Small businesses should be exempt, though they should be able to choose to join the VAT system. Social Security and means-tested government programs, such as Temporary Assistance to Needy Families, should be adjusted to reflect the after-VAT price of relevant purchases.

Border adjustments are ubiquitous in VATs around the world and do not constitute tariffs. And almost all VAT countries exempt small businesses (somehow defined). Limiting the VAT to firms with more than $200,000 in gross receipts would exempt 43 million small businesses.

Finally, the UBI payment would eliminate the burden of the VAT and give additional resources to low- and moderate-income households. My version would set the UBI at the federal poverty line times the VAT rate (10 percent) times two. For example, a family of four

Value-added taxes are a relatively new concept for most Americans, but most countries around the world have them.

would receive about $5,200 per year. My UBI proposal is similar to, but smaller than, the version proposed by Democratic presidential candidate Andrew Yang.

Effects

A 10 percent VAT would raise about $2.9 trillion over 10 years, or 1.1 percent of Gross Domestic Product, even after covering the cost of the UBI.

As with any tax, its effects on the economy would depend on how government uses the revenue. But all else equal, it would be better for the economy (that is, less distortionary) than hiking income tax rates.

To avoid disrupting the economy in the short run, the VAT proceeds should be used in the early years to stimulate the economy, and the Fed should accommodate the VAT by letting the consumer price level rise.

The Tax Policy Center estimates that the VAT in conjunction with a UBI would be extremely progressive. It would increase after-tax income of the lowest-income 20 percent of households by 17 percent. The tax burden for middle-income people would be unchanged while incomes of the top 1 percent of households would fall by 5.5 percent.

It may seem counter-intuitive, but the VAT functions as a 10 percent tax on existing wealth because future consumption can be financed only with existing wealth or future wages. Unlike a tax imposed on accumulated assets, the VAT's implicit wealth tax is very difficult to avoid or evade and does not require the valuation of assets.

A VAT also could benefit states. While states would not have to conform to the new federal law, doing so could improve the structure of their consumption taxes, which tend to exempt services and necessities and often tax businesses. Canada's provinces provide an example of how national and sub-national VATs can "harmonize."

Politics

One hundred sixty-eight countries have a VAT. But would Congress ever pass one? It may not be so far-fetched. In recent years, such a tax (under other names) has been proposed by leading Republicans such as senators Ted Cruz of Texas and Rand Paul of Kentucky, former House Speaker Paul Ryan, and others.

Many years ago, former Treasury Secretary Larry Summers quipped that a VAT has little political support because liberals think it is regressive and conservatives think it is a money machine. He was right.

But liberals should realize that the VAT can be progressive, especially when combined with the UBI. It would be even more progressive if the revenues financed, say, health care or childcare.

There are benefits for conservatives as well. Despite claims to the contrary, there is little evidence that VATs ever increase overall government spending. And in the US, a VAT could be enacted as part of a broader budget agreement that explicitly slows federal spending growth over time.

Ultimately, the real debate will be about how to use the money generated by the VAT. But if new revenues are an inevitable part of any effort to control the federal budget, a VAT with a UBI could be one of the best policy options.

EVALUATING THE AUTHOR'S ARGUMENTS:

Viewpoint author William G. Gale argues that his plan of combining a VAT and universal basic income should appeal to both liberals and conservatives. Does the author make a strong case? Do you agree with him? Why or why not?

Viewpoint

5

History Provides a Grave Warning Against Universal Basic Income

Zilvinas Silenas

"UBI is a very serious issue with the potential to sever the link between effort and reward."

In the following viewpoint, Zilvinas Silenas argues that universal basic income—even in the form of stimulus checks from the government due to the COVID-19 crisis—is a poor solution. The author points to the state of Germany after its defeat in World War I to illustrate the dangers of hyperinflation and the inadequacies of handouts to grow the economy. UBI will dampen the motivation to work, and that, Silenas maintains, is the true danger to the economy. Zilvinas Silenas is president of the Foundation for Economic Education and the former president of the Lithuanian Free Market Institute.

AS YOU READ, CONSIDER THE FOLLOWING QUESTIONS:
1. What historical period does the author compare to the present crisis?
2. How does the author connect stimulus checks with universal basic income?
3. What is the danger of printing additional money?

Massive government debt, sky-high unemployment, the economy frozen, idle workers receiving payments from the government. This might sound like COVID-19, but I am actually talking about post-World War I Germany.

If your high school history teacher skipped this story, here's a bullet-point recap:

- Germany lost World War I in 1918.
- Great Britain and France punished Germany with huge fines.
- Germans resented the fines and defaulted on their payments.
- France got fed up and in 1923 invaded Germany's coal-rich Ruhr valley to extract payments themselves.
- Germans offered nonviolent resistance.
- German coal miners refused to work for the French occupiers, and the German government printed even more money to pay the miners so they could feed themselves and their families.

Fast-forward to 2020. Massive government debt: check. Entire sectors of the economy frozen: check. Large portion of population unable to work: check. Government giving handouts: check. Calls for more handouts: check. Pick any western country and this would be a pretty accurate description of its current state.

Let's continue our history refresher. Remember those old black-and-white pictures of children playing with stacks of money? Or people burning money rather than firewood, because money was cheaper than firewood? That's interwar Germany and as many assume, in the midst of a financial crisis caused by a Wall Street crash.

But these pictures are dated to 1923-1924 and the Wall Street crash didn't happen until 1929. Why the hyperinflation then? As usual, it's complicated. That hyperinflation was a product of many

Printing extra money is not the answer to the problem of a struggling economy.

factors, especially monetary expansion, but printing money to pay workers who refused to work was one. It would be inaccurate to say that these payments were the sole cause of the hyperinflation (many would argue that inflation was already underway even before the French invasion). But, it would probably also be inaccurate to say this played no part in the hyperinflation.

Let's go back to today. Giving people money "just because" is essentially Universal Basic Income (UBI). You can call it "stimulus checks" if you want, but if the one-time payments transformed into monthly payments, at some point you have to admit that the essential discussion is about UBI and not "extraordinary measures."

There are many arguments for and against UBI, but one often overlooked issue is whether or not UBI stimulates the economy. The often-presented case follows a line of reasoning similar to this example: People receive their UBI, they spend that money on hot dogs, the owner of the hot dog stand will then have money to visit a barber, the barber will then have money to buy hot dogs. Call it the "Circle of Life" if you are into "Lion King," or the "Circular Flow" if you are into economics.

But in order to "inject money" into the economy, you have to withdraw it from somewhere. Giving everyone $2,000 would "inject" $8 trillion into the economy, but if you increase taxes to raise that $8 trillion, you would with-

draw money from the economy. You would be achieving redistribution, not stimulus.

Financing UBI by borrowing is another option. But borrowing is essentially using the resources of tomorrow to finance consumption today. You can consume more today at the expense of tomorrow, but that's just saddling future taxpayers with debt.

There is an argument that borrowing should not be of concern because if we invest the borrowed resources right, it will lead to such an explosion of economic growth that repaying the debt will be easy; after all, businesses borrow all the time. But think for a second. How will borrowing money and giving it out to everyone, regardless of what they do, lead to long-term economic or technological breakthroughs?

Finally, there are those who say we should just print money and give it out to everyone. But there's a cemetery of economies full of countries who've tried just that: Zimbabwe, Venezuela, interwar Germany, and even the Roman empire. Economic welfare is not how much money you have, but what you can buy with it. If you continue printing money, sooner or later money will lose value.

Admittedly, there are many factors involved that can mask inflation (e.g. falling oil prices). It could take much longer for the US to get there than interwar Germany, but the basic mechanism is the same.

Some say that inflation is a price worth paying to have everyone employed. But wouldn't people receive UBI regardless of their employment? Unless someone has a logical explanation backed up with some empirics on how giving everyone money—regardless of whether you work or sit on a couch—encourages you to work, it is merely wishful thinking for now.

UBI is no miracle. Those that peddle it are no visionaries or Santas. Those who oppose it are not scrooges. It is a very serious issue with the potential to sever the link between effort and reward. If you worry about the situations where people ask to be fired because living on temporary benefits is better than working, what do you think will happen when we just start handing out money to everyone forever?

EVALUATING THE AUTHOR'S ARGUMENTS:

Viewpoint author Zilvinas Silenas argues that we should look to lessons of the past when creating new policies. The author equates the hyperinflation experienced by post–World War I Germany and stimulus checks provided as COVID-19 pandemic relief packages in the United States with proposals for universal basic income. Is that a fair analogy? Why or why not?

Giving People Money Isn't Easy

Surbhi Bhatia and Vishnu Padmanabhan

"Even if the poor are correctly identified, getting money into their hands can be difficult."

In the following viewpoint, Surbhi Bhatia and Vishnu Padmanabhan argue that in India UBI is too expensive, but basic income could be provided to the poorest part of the population for a reasonable cost. However, implementing a program still has many challenges. It is not always simple to identify people living in poverty, and wealthy people sometimes take money intended for the poor. Surbhi Bhatia is a data expert, and Vishnu Padmanabhan works for the Centre for Effective Governance of Indian States.

AS YOU READ, CONSIDER THE FOLLOWING QUESTIONS:
1. What are the challenges for states wishing to implement UBI at the state level?
2. Why can it be difficult to get money to people living in poverty?
3. When people are given cash, how do they tend to spend it, according to studies cited?

"Can UBI Reignite the Economy?" by Surbhi Bhatia, Vishnu Padmanabhan, HT Media Limited, January 29, 2020. Reprinted by permission.

A mid a consumption slump, several economists have called on the government to "put money into people's hands." Some have even suggested the government do that literally: through unconditional, regular payments to citizens as part of a universal basic income (UBI). But is implementing UBI financially and administratively feasible? And would it even work?

Unlike developed countries, where UBI is being proposed to insulate citizens from the disruption of automation, developing countries view it as a measure to boost income and alleviate poverty. In India, the idea of a national UBI emerged with the 2016–17 Economic Survey. The survey laid out the blueprint for a "quasi" UBI, proposing ₹7,620 per year to 75% of the population. In 2019 prices, this would cost the Indian government around 4.5% of GDP. Since then, others have proposed versions of the same concept that differ significantly in both scope and cost.

Economist Reetika Khera, for instance, has kept women at the centre of her version suggesting that basic income be first transferred to pregnant women, children, the widowed, the elderly and the disabled before being extended to the rest of the population.

In contrast, Maitreesh Ghatak and Karthik Muralidharan have suggested making basic income truly universal and unconditional but cap the total cost to 1% of GDP. This results in smaller monthly transfers (₹110 per person per month) but still significant enough to reduce poverty, improve financial inclusion and boost female empowerment.

Others have approached UBI as an alternative to existing subsidies and government spending. For instance, the International Monetary Fund (IMF) suggested that if subsidies were eliminated, the government could provide all Indians with ₹2,600 (in 2011–12 prices) every month.

Using a similar approach, Mint crunched the numbers to estimate the costs of various versions of UBI. We find that some versions, such as a pure UBI which provides all Indians with ₹1,215 per month (based on the latest estimated poverty line), would be prohibitively expensive (more than 10% of GDP and exceeding the centre's tax revenues). But other versions could be potentially affordable and cost less than 3% of GDP (the potential savings from rolled-back

Should everyone be eligible for UBI, or should it go strictly to those who need it?

subsidies). The Congress brainchild Nyuntam Aay Yojana (NYAY), for example, which proposes ₹6,000 a month to the poorest 20% of households, would cost less than 3% of GDP but would be costly if it had to become universal. Similarly, the Economic Survey proposal could be feasible if it is limited to just poor households—but any larger version would quickly become too expensive.

All these calculations assume a basic income programme implemented nationally and funded entirely by the centre. But the states, too, can take the lead. Telangana's Rhythu Bandhu scheme, for instance, which provides Rs. 8000 per acre per year to landholding farmers, preceded the current national-level farmer cash transfer scheme (PM Kisan). But for states to implement a larger-scale UBI on their own could be difficult. For instance, a basic income pegged at a state's poverty line and targeting the state's poor would significantly eat into state expenditures and poorer states would bear the greater burden (e.g. it would cost Bihar nearly 20% of its state GDP). Consequently, almost all proposed UBI programmes have incorporated a cost-sharing mechanism between the centre and state governments.

But even if states and centres do find the finances, implementation is a challenge. For a start, identifying the poor in India has been a perennial problem. Programmes and subsidies designed for the poor often end up being dispropor-tionately used by the rich. An increasingly popular solution is to use the data from the Socio-Economic Caste Census (SECC) to exclude obviously ineligible beneficiaries. The Economic Survey's UBI proposal suggested excluding beneficiaries based on SECC data on asset ownership (e.g. cars or air-conditioners). But even this system is not fool-proof. SECC data, collected in 2011, is now dated but there are also questions around its accuracy.

Moreover, even if the poor are correctly identified, getting money into their hands can be difficult. Despite a national push to increase the coverage of bank accounts among the poor, usage of bank accounts remains weak. For instance, the World Bank's World Findex Survey found a big gap between account ownership and usage in India. Nearly 80% of adults owned an account in 2017 but almost half of these accounts were inactive (no deposit or withdrawal in the previous year). This gap is even higher for the poorest 40% of the population.

These considerable fiscal and administrative challenges could explain why there have been only a handful of UBI experiments across the world. Consequently, many questions about UBI remain unanswered. By definition, any version of UBI will immediately increase incomes but less is known about the long-term effects on local markets and the economy. Evaluations of other cash transfer programmes, though, hint at the promise of UBI. According to one review, studies across the world have shown that giving people cash does not result in the commonly perceived negative effects. When given cash, people do not waste it on alcohol or drugs and neither are they less inclined to work. Instead, they seem to, depending on their circumstances, spend it on different items ranging from food to education to assets. In India, then, where the poor face varied constraints and financial volatility, a large-scale UBI-type programme may be one way to smooth consumption, alleviate poverty and give the economy the demand boost it needs.

EVALUATING THE AUTHORS' ARGUMENTS:

Viewpoint authors Surbhi Bhatia and Vishnu Padmanabhan address some of the substantial challenges of implementing UBI in India. Do you think similar challenges would exist in the United States? Why or why not?

Facts About Universal Basic Income

Editor's note: These facts can be used in reports to add credibility when making important points or claims.

What Is Universal Basic Income (UBI)?

Full universal basic income would be a regular transfer of money to every citizen in a country. The money is paid regardless of income, employment, need, or other factors. The money is given as cash (including electronic transfers), with no rules about how it can be used. Every adult receives the same amount, although people with additional income may lose some or all of the UBI through taxes. Children may or may not be given the same amounts as adults.

The goal of UBI is to eliminate poverty and reduce inequality. It takes away the stigma of receiving targeted support, such as food stamps and child assistance programs. It also reduces the paperwork and oversight needed for those programs.

Millions of full-time workers earn wages that put them below the poverty line in the US. Over half of these workers are people of color. The percent of full-time workers who are economically insecure has increased significantly since 2000, according to Policy Link, a national research and action institute. UBI could reduce this inequality.

What Are the Pros and Cons of UBI?

Divakar Shenoy covered the arguments in "UBI: The Good, the Bad, and the Complicated" in the first viewpoint of chapter 1. The following are the advantages:

First, UBI would give individuals freedom to spend the money in a way they choose. In other words, UBI strengthens economic liberty at an individual level. This would help them to choose the kind of work they want to do, rather than forcing them to do unproductive work to meet their daily requirements.

Universal basic income would be a sort of insurance against unemployment and hence help in reducing poverty.

UBI will result in an equitable distribution of wealth. As explained previously, only the poor will receive the full net benefits.

Increased income will increase the bargaining power of individuals, as they will no longer be forced to accept any working conditions.

UBI is easy to implement. Because of its universal character, there is no need to identify the beneficiaries. Thus it excludes errors in identifying the intended beneficiaries—which is a common problem in targeted welfare schemes.

As every individual receives basic income, it promotes efficiency by reducing wastages in government transfers. This would also help in reducing corruption.

Considerable gains could be achieved in terms of bureaucratic costs and time by replacing many of the social sector schemes with UBI.

As an economic survey points out, transferring basic income directly into bank accounts will increase the demand for financial services. This would help banks to invest in the expansion of their service network, which is very important for financial inclusion.

Under some circumstances, UBI could promote greater productivity. For example, agriculture laborers who own a small patch of land and earlier used to work on others' farms for low wages can now undertake farming on their own land. In the long term, this will reduce the percentage of unused land and help in increasing agriculture productivity.

The following are the challenges:

A guaranteed minimum income might make people lazy and breed dependency. They may opt out of the labor market.

There is no guarantee that the additional income will be spent on education, health care, etc., and money could be spent on "temptation goods," such as alcohol, tobacco, drugs, etc.

Given the large population size, the fiscal burden on government would be high. Also, as Economic Survey 2016–17 noted, once implemented, it may become difficult for the government to end UBI in the case of failure.

If the UBI is funded by higher taxes, especially by indirect taxes, it will result in inflation. This, in turn, will reduce the purchasing power of people and lower the value of the amount transferred.

A "guaranteed minimum income" might reduce the availability of workers in some sectors that are necessary but unattractive and raise the wages of such work. For example, the wages of agriculture laborers might increase due to non-availability of workers willing to work on others' farms.

How Do Americans Feel About UBI?

A 2017 poll by Gallup found 48% of American adults supported UBI and 52% did not. A Zogby Strategies poll found 40% in favor of UBI, 35% opposed, and 25% undecided. The 2019 Understanding America Study survey found 37% supported UBI, 40% were opposed, and 23% had no opinion. All these surveys took place before the COVID-19 pandemic put millions of people out of work, which may have changed opinions on UBI.

Support from the political right is limited, and those conservatives who do show interest in UBI want to fund UBI by cutting all other government assistance. This could mean far smaller benefits to people in poverty. It is easier to find political support for programs such as food stamps and early childhood education. Many Americans do not want money to go to healthy adults who are not working.

Organizations to Contact

The editors have compiled the following list of organizations concerned with the issues debated in this book. The descriptions are derived from materials provided by the organizations. All have publications or information available for interested readers. The list was compiled on the date of publication of the present volume; the information provided here may change. Be aware that many organizations take several weeks or longer to respond to inquiries, so allow as much time as possible for the receipt of requested materials.

The American Enterprise Institute for Public Policy Research
1789 Massachusetts Avenue NW
Washington, DC 20036
(202) 862-5800
email: AcademicPrograms@aei.org
website: www.aei.org/
This think tank researches government, politics, economics, and social welfare. Areas of interest include economic mobility, tax reform, and the economics of health care and education.

ATD Fourth World
12 rue Pasteur
95480 Pierrelaye
France
contact: www.atd-fourthworld.org/contact/
website: www.atd-fourthworld.org/
ATD Fourth World is a nonprofit organization that aims to eradicate chronic poverty through a human-rights based approach. It publishes books, journals, reports, and videos to help understand extreme poverty.

Basic Income Canada Network

723-1500 Bank Street
Ottawa, ON K1H 1B8
email: info@basicincomecanada.org
website: basicincomecanada.org
A nonprofit organization composed of people interested in income issues. The organization connects individuals, institutions, and groups; raises awareness about basic income; and attempts to influence policy. The website includes facts about basic income, introductory and in-depth reading, podcasts, and videos.

The Brookings Institution

1775 Massachusetts Avenue NW
Washington, DC 20036
(202) 797-6000
email: communications@brookings.edu
website: www.brookings.edu
This nonprofit public policy organization conducts research "that leads to new ideas for solving problems facing society at the local, national and global level."

Center on Budget and Policy Priorities (CBPP)

1275 First Street NE, Suite 1200
Washington, DC 20002
(202) 408-1080
email: center@cbpp.org
website: www.cbpp.org/
This progressive American think tank analyzes the impact of federal and state government budget policies.

The Citizen's Basic Income Trust

106 Queens Road
Buckhurst Hill
United Kingdom
IG9 5BS

email: info@citizensincome.org
website: citizensincome.org/
This organization promotes debate on the desirability and feasibility
of UBI. It publishes a newsletter and other publications and has a
library of resources.

Hoover Institution
434 Galvez Mall, Stanford University
Stanford, CA 94305-6003
(650) 723-1754

Hoover Institution in Washington, The Johnson Center
1399 New York Avenue NW, Suite 500
Washington, DC 20005
(202) 760-3200

email: sfarley@stanford.edu
website: www.hoover.org/
The Hoover Institution "seeks to improve the human condition by
advancing ideas that promote economic opportunity and prosperity,
while securing and safeguarding peace for America and all mankind."

Tax Foundation
1325 G Street NW
Suite 950
Washington, DC 20005
(202) 464-6200
contact form: taxfoundation.org/contact/
website: taxfoundation.org/
The Tax Foundation is an independent tax policy nonprofit. Its goal
is to "improve lives through tax policies that lead to greater economic
growth and opportunity." The website provides information on a
variety of taxes and new tax proposals.

The Universal Income Project
(202) 713-5665
email: questions@universalincome.org
website: www.universalincome.org/
This group is dedicated to implementing UBI in America. It organizes "Basic Income Create-a-Thons" to build awareness and support for UBI.

World Basic Income
99 Minehead Avenue
Manchester
United Kingdom
M20 1EP
email: info@worldbasicincome.org.uk
website: www.worldbasicincome.org.uk/
This organization supports UBI worldwide in order to redistribute money. It states, "A world basic income would redistribute money to achieve greater social justice and to secure each individual's right to life."

For Further Reading

Books

Dean, Hartley. *Understanding Human Need*. Bristol, UK: Policy Press, 2020. The author discusses the nature of human need and the ethical principles associated with being human. This background is used to discuss welfare programs and UBI.

Haagh, Louise. *The Case for Universal Basic Income*. Cambridge, UK: Polity, 2019. One of the world's leading experts on basic income argues that UBI is essential to freedom, human development, and democracy.

Miller, Annie. *A Basic Income Handbook*. Edinburgh, UK: Luath Press, 2017. The author combines personal reflections and research into a feminist argument in favor of UBI.

Pettinger, Lynne. *What's Wrong with Work?* Bristol, UK: Policy Press, 2019. The author explores work in economic, political, and social terms and considers the effect commerce has on the environment. This discussion could act as a background for debating the necessity of making everyone work for money.

Standing, Guy. *Basic Income: And How We Can Make It Happen*. New York, NY: Penguin, 2017. A long-time proponent of UBI explores the effects it might have on the economy, poverty, work, and labor. He "disproves the standard arguments against Basic Income; explains what we can learn from pilots across the world and illustrates exactly why a Basic Income has now become such an urgent necessity."

Torry, Malcolm. *The Feasibility of Citizen's Income (Exploring the Basic Income Guarantee)*. New York, NY: Palgrave Macmillan, 2016. This book considers the financial possibilities of UBI as well as psychological, political, and administrative challenges.

Torry, Malcolm, editor. *The Palgrave International Handbook of Basic Income*. New York, NY: Palgrave Macmillan, 2019. This handbook looks at the debates on UBI and compares pilot projects from around the world.

Torry, Malcolm. *Why We Need a Citizen's Basic Income: The Desirability, Feasibility and Implementation of an Unconditional Income.* Bristol, UK: Policy Press, 2018. The author examines possible ways UBI could be implemented and considers the costs. He includes examples from countries around the world.

Wehner, Burkhard. *Universal Basic Income and the Reshaping of Democracy: Towards a Citizen's Stipend in a New Political Order.* Heidelberg, Germany: Springer, 2019. In this 60-page essay, the author argues that people in favor of UBI have not spent enough time considering how it would be financed.

Periodicals and Internet Sources

Acemoglu, Daron, "Opinion: Why Universal Basic Income Is a bad Idea," MarketWatch, June 19, 2019. https://www.marketwatch.com /story/why-universal-basic-income-is-a-bad-idea-2019-06-19

Amadeo, Kimberly. "Universal Basic Income, Its Pros and Cons with Examples," The Balance, December 13, 2019. https://www .thebalance.com/universal-basic-income-4160668

Arnold, Carrie, "Money for Nothing: The Truth About Universal Basic Income," *Nature*, May 30, 2018. https://www.nature.com/articles /d41586-018-05259-x

Coelho, Andre, "Basic Income: Exit Strategy or Exit Trap?" Basic Income Earth Network, February 11, 2020. https://basicincome.org /news/2020/02/basic-income-exit-strategy-or-exit-trap/

Howgego, Joshua, "Universal Income Study Finds Money for Nothing Won't Make Us Work Less," New Scientist Ltd., February 8, 2019. https://www.newscientist.com/article/2193136-universal-income -study-finds-money-for-nothing-wont-make-us-work-less/

Jones, Brad, "Experts Say a Universal Basic Income Would Boost US Economy by Staggering $2.5 Trillion," Futurism, November 27, 2017. https://futurism.com/experts-universal-basic -income-boost-us-economy-staggering-2-5-trillion

Linares, Julio, "Basic Income World Wide Survey," Basic Income Earth Network, August 4, 2020. https://basicincome.org/news/2020/08 /basic-income-world-wide-survey/

Maira, Arun, "Opinion: Good Jobs, Not Universal Basic Income, Are Needed for a Good Society," Live Mint, March 10, 2020. https://www.livemint.com/opinion/online-views/opinion-good-jobs-not-universal-basic-income-are-needed-for-a-good-society-1551203819140.html

Martinelli, Luke, "Basic Income: World's First National Experiment in Finland Shows Only Modest Benefits," The Conversation, February 22, 2019. https://theconversation.com/basic-income-worlds-first-national-experiment-in-finland-shows-only-modest-benefits-111391

McQuillan, Lawrence, and Rebecca Sklar, "The Solution for 'Robogeddon' Is Rapid Retraining, Not Guaranteed Income," The Hill, August 24, 2018. https://thehill.com/opinion/technology/403092-the-solution-for-robogeddon-is-rapid-retraining-notguaranteed-income

Parker, Clifton B. "Stanford Scholar Explores Pros, Cons of 'Basic Income,'" Stanford News, August 8, 2018. https://news.stanford.edu/2018/08/08/stanford-scholar-explores-pros-cons-basic-income/

ProCon.org, "Universal Basic Income—Top 3 Pros and Cons," September 18, 2017. https://www.procon.org/headline.php?headlineID=005363

Standing, Guy, "Universal Basic Income Is Becoming an Urgent Necessity," Guardian News and Media Limited, January 12, 2017. https://www.theguardian.com/commentisfree/2017/jan/12/universal-basic-income-finland-uk

Stone, Chad, "A Universal Basic Income Is No Solution," U.S. News & World Report, June 3, 2016. https://www.usnews.com/opinion/articles/2016-06-03/a-universal-basic-income-wouldnt-reduce-poverty

Torry, Malcolm, "An Article on Basic Income Funded by Sovereign Money," Basic Income Earth Network, July 9, 2020. https://basicincome.org/news/2020/07/an-article-on-basic-income-funded-by-sovereign-money/

Ziobrowska, Justyna, "Universal Basic Income," EconClips, 2018. https://econclips.com/universal-basic-income-pros-and-cons-ubi/

Websites

The Basic Income Earth Network (BIEN) (www.basicincomeaction .org/) Founded in 1986, BIEN links individuals and groups interested in basic income and tries to foster informed discussion on the topic throughout the world. The website includes FAQs, links to research, and opinion polls.

US Basic Income Guarantee Network (USBIG) (www.usbig.net) USBIG is a volunteer nonprofit group dedicated to increasing discussion on basic income. It provides a monthly newsletter, videos, resource links, and a blog series.

The Wharton Public Policy Initiative (repository.upenn.edu /pennwhartonppi_home/) This is a hub for public policy research and education from the University of Pennsylvania.

Index

Picture Credits

Cover stefanphotozemun/Shutterstock.com; p. 10 yurii_zym/iStock/ Getty Images Plus; pp. 14, 61 Spencer Platt/Getty Images; p. 21 Thomas Niedermueller/Getty Images; p. 27 Education Images/ Universal Images Group via Getty Images; p. 33 Tolga Akmen/AFP via Getty Images; p. 37 Alex Garcia/Chicago Tribune/Tribune News Service via Getty Images; p. 42 Kena Betancur/Getty Images; p. 45 Lars Baron/Getty Images; p. 53 Ringo Chiu/Getty Images; p. 65 Jon Feingersh Photography Inc./DigitalVision/Getty Images; p. 71 Monica Murphy/Moment/Getty Images; p. 74 Drew Angerer/Getty Images; p. 81 Louisa Gouliamaki/AFP via Getty Images; p. 87 RomanR/ Shutterstock.com; p. 93 Thiam/Shutterstock.com,; p. 98 vipman/ Shutterstock.com; p. 103 BRO Vector/iStock/Getty Images.